ORGANIZE YOUR START-UP!

ORGANIZE YOUR START-UP!

SIMPLE METHODS TO HELP YOU START THE BUSINESS OF YOUR DREAMS

RONNI EISENBERG WITH KATE KELLY

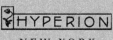

HYPERION

NEW YORK

Library of Congress Cataloging-in-Publication Data

Eisenberg, Ronni.
  Organize your start-up! : simple methods to help you start the business of your dreams / Ronni Eisenberg with Kate Kelly.
    p. cm.
  ISBN 0-7868-8625-0
  1. New business enterprises. I. Kelly, Kate. II. Title.

HD62.5.E399 2001
658.1'1—dc21

00–049897

FIRST EDITION

10 9 8 7 6 5 4 3 2 1

CONTENTS

INTRODUCTION

Starting your own business is an exciting prospect. You're in for a real adventure—and a roller-coaster ride in the process.

There are few things that offer such an excellent opportunity for both business and personal growth. You'll test yourself both mentally and physically as you draw up a business plan, figure out how to finance your venture, select a location (whether it's in your home or out in the community), take care of the legalities of starting a business, establish an office, hire staff (if necessary), set up financial and accounting procedures, work out a marketing plan, create a Web site (most businesses need a presence on the Web), and then figure out how this is all going to make money.

It's exhausting and exhilarating. There will be days when you're ready to tear out your hair, and days when you'll be as proud as you can be that you're making it on your own.

There are two pieces of advice I want to share with you now because you'll need them as you go through the process:

1. **If the research about the business potential of your venture looks promising, don't let others dissuade you.**

   Parents, spouses, relatives, and friends sometimes want you to do the "safe" thing by keeping your job. While there are times in life when all of us must stay in a position with a steady paycheck, you must also keep searching for the time when you can afford to "test your wings." Life is never "perfect" for a business launch, but with planning and saving, you should be able to make the leap into self-employment when the time is right. (And as you'll read, there are many tasks you can do while still employed that will keep your business dream moving forward.)

When I started my organizing business 23 years ago, many people had difficulty understanding the concept of what I wanted to do. Though an entire national organization of professional organizers exists now, at the time I was starting out there were fewer than a dozen people who were offering time management and organizational advice. My friends kept asking doubtfully, "How will you get people to hire you?" "What exactly will you *do* for the person if they do hire you?" "How much do you think someone would pay you for that?" "How long will the work take?" Answers to all those questions had to be explored first-hand.

I had faith in myself and faith in the fact that my services were needed. (How often had people said to me, "Boy, could I use you"?) I also had the *drive* and the *tenacity* to make it work. In addition, you need a *pioneering spirit* and the willingness to *work hard*.

Now—23 years later—it gives me great pride to look back and to realize that several of us gave birth to an entire industry— one for which there is an ever-increasing need, I might add!

From my story and countless others you'll hear as you meet other business owners, you'll learn that if you let the naysayers get you down, you'll never know if you could have succeeded or not. Keep going. You can do it.

This brings me to the second piece of advice I have for you—one that relates directly to my business:

2. You have to stay organized or you'll lose control of what you're working so hard to achieve.

While there are other books that talk about starting a business, my book provides you with something vital to business success: **an organized mind-set.**

Lots of people have good ideas. A good number of people have the ability to get a business up and running. Only an organized few see their businesses succeed. (Only about 20 percent of small businesses started today will exist in five years.)

Many people who start their own businesses have to be their own sales force, telephone receptionist, office manager, business location scout, Web master, accountant, computer expert, mail sorter, secretary, publicist, spokesperson, ad executive, janitor, street cleaner (for those with storefronts), and CEO. To juggle so many roles, you must have methods for tracking what is happening in every aspect of your business.

Calendar notations, a running "to do" list, daily priority lists, excellent files, organized methods of following up with sales leads and other business contacts, and a well-planned investment in office equipment that "does the work for you" are now going to be a very important part of your life.

That's where this book will come in handy. In addition to providing what you need to know about starting and running a business, I give you added insight about how to do it in an organized and efficient way.

HOW TO USE THIS BOOK

The chapters are sequential, organized in such a way that you can proceed through them step by step, or if you already have taken care of certain aspects of getting started, you can go through the book selectively.

You may also want to use the book as a "refresher" course. Perhaps you're putting all your energy into getting your retail store ready for a grand opening. Later on, you may want to devote time to getting a Web page established. Come back to the book and review the necessary chapter at that time.

All books in this "organizing" series are written so that they can be used as checklists that provide guidance on what you need to do. Go ahead and write in the book—you'll find it more helpful if you keep track of the "done" and "not done" right here where the task is described. But most important, let this book be your guide as you watch your idea grow from a dream to a successful reality.

PART ONE

GETTING STARTED

1

BEFORE YOU QUIT YOUR "DAY" JOB

WHAT'S AHEAD

Why Start a Business?
Choose Carefully
Define Your Business
Is a Franchise for You?
Define Your Market
Establish a Timetable
Resolve the Key Business Owner Issue
Locating Money
Establish Your "Red Flag" Level
Consider Your Qualifications

"**I** want to start a business" are words that have been uttered by countless numbers of men and women. The dream of working for yourself—running a store, visiting clients as a consultant, or setting up an Internet company—is very seductive: interesting challenges, the potential of great money, and the pleasure of not having to answer to anyone else. All together, self-employment is an attractive option.

The catch is that it involves a lot of hard work. Before you take the plunge, it's vital to do some serious planning so that your business venture will grow and succeed.

WHY START A BUSINESS?

"Because I really want to" is the only truly satisfactory reason for starting a business. Running your own business requires a huge amount of time, energy, and emotional push, and positive financial results may come in ten months or ten years. It's not an easy thing to do and should never be undertaken because you lost your job and didn't know what else to do, or because you "kind of wanted to." You need to *really* want to, as it's going to require a huge amount of your time from this day forth.

To begin with, you need to do your homework.

CHOOSE CAREFULLY

Most people who buy a book like this do so with a dream in mind. If you're still casting about for the "perfect" idea, here are a few tips to help you narrow the field:

- Stay with what you know. While you can certainly break away from your current profession, you'll enjoy it more and be better prepared to run a business that focuses on something that is familiar to you. The dog day-care business for a pet lover is workable as is the antique shop for the collector, but if you hate to read, stay away from a bookstore.

- Do you have some basic knowledge of the other tasks that will be a part of running the type of business you're considering? The former manager of a men's clothing store is well-prepared to run another type of retail operation. The psychologist who wants to set up a counseling center but has never dealt with any aspect of business has some homework to do before she goes out on her own.

- Does the type of business suit your long-term needs? The person who loves being with his family should stay far away from the restaurant business, where the busiest times are late in the day and the busiest days are on the weekend. Don't fool yourself into thinking you'll soon reach the point where you can hire others to do what you don't like to do. Unfortunately, the less desirable jobs may be ones you have to reabsorb now and then for the remainder of the life of the business.

- Does the idea of this particular business excite you? Whether you're importing baskets from France or selling art over the Internet, you need to have an enthusiasm for the business that will see you through good times and bad.

DEFINE YOUR BUSINESS

"I want to start an Internet company."

"I think I'll become a consultant."

"There's affordable space on Main Street. I think I'll start a store."

These are all possible first sentences—good starts—for what needs to be a defining paragraph about your company. You need to clarify exactly what your product and service is, who will be interested in it, and why they will buy. In the process, you will define what is unique about your business.

Hanging out your shingle is only part of the process of starting your own business. Before you open your door, you need to know exactly what will be going on in the "storefront" inside:

- Develop a very clear image of what your business will be like. Deciding to be "the best" isn't good enough. You need to be more specific:

— The Internet entrepreneur can't just start a Web site; it has to be a specialized Web site, such as one that offers information to parents of twins, or a site that sells every size and style of ball.

— The consultant must consult on something specific. Whether it's how to advertise on the Internet or how to invest money, you need to offer advice on something people need or want to know about.

— And instead of opening a hardware store, define what type of hardware store it will be. Perhaps you decide yours will be a store carrying high-priced specialty tools and equipment rather than ordinary hammers and nails.

Now you have a concept that can grow into a business.

• Visualize exactly what your workday might be like. Do you see yourself consulting on global warming, running a local children's clothing store, or teaching people how to get their dogs to obey?

• Where will you perform the type of task you visualize? Knowing whether you'll be with people constantly or on your own most of the time will make a difference in deciding whether this is the right business for you.

The more specific your business goal, the easier it will be to make that dream come true.

IS A FRANCHISE FOR YOU?

A franchise offers the advantage of a preplanned business complete with a product (or service) and experience-based know-how on how to sell it. For the required fee the franchise company will help you establish your business. Tying in with a franchise also makes it easier to obtain money because there is value inherent in connecting with a good franchise: While a ma-and-pa music store might go belly up and no one would particularly notice, a good franchise will stay behind the people they've permitted to buy into the organization, so a bank or an investor is taking less risk with you if you've connected with a franchise.

However, franchises are confining and may offer some of the negative aspects of working for someone else. To maintain the integrity of the franchise, the franchisor limits the product line, approves the ingredients of any food-related creation, and oversees the quality of your operation. As a result, you need to follow directions (creativity does upset them), and you will be supervised, more so at first and less so as your relationship continues.

DEFINE YOUR MARKET

Who is your customer? "Anyone and everyone" is the wrong answer. You need to target your market. A party planner could decide to organize events for corporations (major parties, conventions, etc.) or for families (fiftieth anniversary parties, Sweet Sixteens, bar/bas mitzvahs, and weddings). By focusing on one type of customer or the other, she'll find that it's easier to promote and run her business.

- Identify exactly to whom you expect to sell your product or service. This will shape your business in more ways than you can ever imagine.

- See Chapter 14 for more information on identifying your market.

ESTABLISH A TIMETABLE

When do you want to start your business? As you'll read in this book, there are many tasks that can be done—and often need to be done—before you're up and running. If you're just beginning to think through your business concept, you may want to set a target date of six months to a year or more. If you want to be a nutritionist but have not yet achieved your certification, you have certain goals to accomplish before you can even consider taking on clients. However, if

---

you've been working as a graphic artist and want to set up a shop of your own, you may already have clients who intend to use you. In this case, a start date could be much sooner.

- Set a target date for when you would like to "open up shop."
- Note down any goals that must be met prior to your start-up and the dates by which you'd like to achieve them (special certification, etc.).

RESOLVE THE KEY BUSINESS OWNER ISSUE

Some people want to start a business with a partner or several partners. You may want to link up with your sister because not only is she your sister, but she's an accounting whiz who is well-prepared to manage the business end of things. Or you may want to set up a law office and bring in other attorneys who offer different expertise.

- Decide whether you want to start a business alone or with other people.
- If you opt to include others, consider their qualifications and personalities very carefully. Running a business with another person is very much like being married—you want to be certain the person is as committed as you are and won't abandon you if the start-up doesn't go exactly as planned.

- Read and follow the advice in Chapter 3, and consult an attorney. You'll need to spell out the relationship very carefully. A good agreement will also stipulate the terms under which the partnership can be dissolved and will explain exactly how it will happen.

LOCATING MONEY

Financing your business is one half of this equation; supporting yourself and your family while you're getting started is the other.

Finding money for your business is discussed in Chapter 8, but for now, it's important to consider how you're going to pay your personal bills while waiting for your business to become profitable. If your business can be run from your home, your financial risks are less than if you need to rent space or purchase inventory. However, the business run out of your home can be closed relatively quickly if the market dries up and you need to take a paying job. The business that requires leasing outside space and investing in equipment and supplies means that you need to be particularly well-funded personally and professionally, because it will be harder to extricate yourself if you need to close the doors.

If you are married, then this issue should be discussed with your spouse; if you're single, then you need to work out how you are going to manage initially and how you would handle personal finances if business slows for a time.

A few fortunate souls have a spouse who is willing to give them the time and the freedom to start a business without having to contribute to the family income right away. Occasionally, a dad with a great business idea will opt to stay home with the kids and shoulder home and new business responsibilities while his wife brings in a steady income.

A good number of businesses are started by stay-at-home mothers who start their businesses slowly as their child-care responsibilities lighten. In this case, any money earned is money the family wouldn't have had, and that offers an obvious advantage.

Otherwise, most people continue their regular "day" jobs until they begin to see both promise and some income from their start-up. While you can't open a retail store and work for someone else full time, there are many types of businesses that can be started nights and weekends. Graphic design, landscape design, legal work, writing, organizing, some types of consulting, as well as starting a Web site, can all be done part-time before losing your steady income. Or suppose you think there's money to be made in exterminating, asbestos removal, cabinetry design and construction, or creating a line of children's clothing—these could be done around your current work schedule. Offering your services at nontraditional times (traditional being nine to five, Monday through Friday) may actually have its benefits. If someone wants an exterminator or to have asbestos removed, they may actually prefer that you come at an off-hour when they can be home to let you in. (How often have you heard people complain about having to take a day off to let the refrigerator repairman come during *his* working hours?)

The next step involves examining your annual budget. Before making the leap to full-time self-employment, make sure that you have work/income on the horizon in your new venture. In addition, you should aspire to have six to nine months of emergency money set aside just for personal use. *This money should be earmarked for personal use only; do not dip into it to bail out the business during a rough time.* To calculate the minimum you should save, consider these expenses:

Home operation
   Rent or mortgage payments   _____
   Maintenance costs   _____

Utilities
   Gas and electricity   _____
   Water/sewer   _____
   Telephone   _____
   Garbage   _____

Loan payments   _____

Credit card payments   _____

Family maintenance

Food   _____

Clothing   _____

Medicine and health costs   _____

Child care   _____

Tuition/lessons   _____

Books/supplies   _____

Personal (haircuts, etc.)   _____

Allowances   _____

Dry cleaning   _____

Lunches (work)   _____

Automobile/transportation

Gas   _____

Maintenance   _____

Parking/public transit   _____

Insurance

Auto   _____

Disability   _____

Health   _____

Homeowners   _____

Life   _____

Long-term care   _____

Miscellaneous
    Alimony   _____
    Dependent support   _____

Taxes
    Federal   _____
    State/local   _____
    Social Security (self-employed)   _____
    Real estate/other   _____

If you have expenses in any of the above categories, these generally constitute your fixed costs—the bills you have to pay in order to maintain your current lifestyle. While you can certainly try to trim your dry cleaning bill, your loan officer will look unfavorably upon receiving less than he is due each month.

In addition to the above, all of us also have miscellaneous expenses, and while most of these expenses are more flexible than those listed above, you may still need to create a category for them: gifts, entertainment, hobbies, vacations, contributions, books/magazines/newspapers, alcohol/tobacco, etc.

Once you have calculated your monthly expenses, multiply those by six (months)—those who are starting riskier ventures should multiply by nine. This gives you the sum of money you need to set aside in case your business enters some dry months.

If you receive regular income from rental property or from Aunt Hilda's estate, then this reduces the amount of money you need to set aside each month.

$ $ $

As you calculate your personal as well as your business finances, keep in mind that it is not unusual to have to continue to invest in the business for 18 to 24 months before being able to take out much more than a small salary for yourself.

ESTABLISH YOUR "RED FLAG" LEVEL

Right now, with your savings balance and your financial information in front of you, establish your "low"—the point at which your finances drop so low that you will need to reevaluate. People who worry a great deal about financial security will likely be uncomfortable when two months' worth of emergency savings are gone; others may be able to tolerate burning through four months' worth of emergency money while trying to get the business going. Decide your "red flag" level of discomfort, and resolve that when the red flag goes up for you, you'll go out and look for paying employment until you are able to resume your efforts.

CONSIDER YOUR QUALIFICATIONS

Now that you have gotten this far, you're ready to plot out the next six months to a year of your life. Most people still need to stockpile some cash and/or look for business financing, and while doing so, it's important to be working in other ways toward your goal of getting your business up and running. Consider:

- Do you need additional certification or a degree in order to be properly qualified for what you want to do? If so, your next step is doing what you need to in order to accomplish that goal.

- Is there any type of work experience that would be beneficial? If you're hoping to buy a franchise for a bread store, you may want to take a job working in some type of retail food establishment or a bakery. By obtaining firsthand experience, you'll stockpile knowledge that will be helpful to you in running your own business. One such franchise has new owners visit another franchise owner and work in their store for a week; later, an experienced store owner comes to visit the new owners to provide additional on-the-job training. You can mimic this type of training by creating your own "apprenticeship" in your chosen field.

    If you've defined your business and taken necessary precautions, you can breathe easy and proceed to formulate plans for what can be a very successful venture.

KEEP IT SIMPLE

1. Take time to plan out your business carefully, and develop a clear image of what your business is to be.

2. Set interim deadlines for tasks you need to accomplish prior to going out on your own.

3. Be certain you've set aside money for six to nine months for personal expenses. Start-ups are costly and may not be profitable for a time.

2
YOUR BUSINESS PLAN

WHAT'S AHEAD

Two Types of Plans
What to Do About Bad News
The Business/Annual Plan
What an Investor or Banker Looks For
The Final Copy

Like a well-marked map, a good business plan shows a new business owner how to reach his or her destination. The primary purpose for creating a business plan is to have a document that will help gain financing. However, by no means is this the only reason for preparing one. It's a very useful tool. As a consultant who specializes in helping people get organized so they can get things done, I'm going to urge you to do a business plan whether or not you need outside investors. My reasoning is simple:

The people whom I see who function well and make their dreams a reality are those who take the time to really think through their plans. The process of writing everything down aids in examining and evaluating your business ideas. Those people who act impulsively and fail to get organized are those who are most likely to have to give up their venture before they really want to.

The business plan offers you an opportunity to do some strategic planning about your long-term goals for the company and the short-term steps that will get you there. The process itself will illuminate potential pitfalls and any weaknesses you need to overcome, and the plan will keep you on target by providing you with a document to refer to when you feel you may be going astray.

Despite how very important it is that you take time to do this planning, most people don't do it because they feel overwhelmed. Please don't skip this chapter. My line of organizing books are successful because they present information in a way that is accessible to readers, and the same will be true here: *This will be the one busi-*

ness plan that even a procrastinator will find easy and relatively painless to do.

TWO TYPES OF PLANS

What is the objective of your plan? This will make a difference as to what type of plan you write. If you are preparing it so that you have a map for guiding your start-up, then this is called an *annual plan*. A *business plan* is what is used to raise capital. The contents are essentially the same; the difference is the audience. The annual plan will be read by you and any other insiders and can be written with that in mind. The business plan must be carefully geared to outsiders, and needs to present honest information that might encourage them to back you financially.

The business plan must be both honest and interesting—interesting because if you are using it to solicit money, you want it to be intriguing, well written, and easy to understand. However, unlike a brochure you might write about your product or service, the only glowing words that should be used are those that can be backed by hard facts and statistical analysis. People who put up money for new ventures need and want to know the truth. If the truth is good, they may put up the money you want them to.

WHAT TO DO ABOUT BAD NEWS

As you go through the following process, you may uncover bad news. Your research may reveal that the competition is vast; it may show that at the price you hoped to charge, you can't make money; it may reveal that the reason there are no competitors in the field is because others have tried and have resoundingly proven that no one wants your product. (A birdhouse that emits bird calls *seemed* like such a good idea . . .)

Despite the fact that getting bad news is always painful, consider yourself spared. Though you've invested time, and perhaps money if you needed a consultant on any aspect of your plan, you've been spared the true pain of starting a business that fails.

With that in mind, the research you've done may well pave the way to another, better idea. Your dream of having your business can still be a reality. Based on what you've learned, you can now refocus your business idea so that it will be more successful.

THE BUSINESS/ANNUAL PLAN

These are the elements of a written plan:

1. **The Summary.** While this—and a table of contents—will be placed first, it should be written last, because it must highlight all of the other elements described below.

2. **Business Description.** This is your mission statement and will include some of the defining points you identified in Chapter 1. It is the "why I started my business and who is my market" section. Within it, you need to specify the types of products you are selling and what your pricing strategy will be. If you're running a home-based business then a description of the location isn't necessary. However, if being near an office complex is key to your lunchtime restaurant business, be certain to include information about the space you're leasing for your business.

   The description should be written in such a way that a potential investor understands what you intend to do so well that she could answer for you if someone were to ask, "So what's this business all about?"

   This is also the place to stress what makes your business better than the competition. Why will your children's clothing store do better than the previous one? Why will someone call your company instead of a competitor if they need a landscape designer? Sometimes the special aspect of your business has to do with your concept for marketing it, in which case the manner in which you intend to sell ready-made dinners (from a cart at the train station?) is important.

If you are seeking funding for your business, then this section should also describe what is happening with your business right now:

- What form of business is it—sole proprietorship, corporation, etc.? (See Chapter 3.)

- Are you already doing business? If not, what is your start date?

- Have you rented space?

- Have you hired staff?

- Have you completed market research and planning? This will be described in detail later in the plan, but for now, report on its status (done, in progress, etc.).

Re: products:

- What is the source of the product?

- If you're manufacturing something, are details worked out for it to be done? In what quantities?

3. **The Market.** For this section of the plan, you need to have gathered some facts. Noting that you think that "most of the town"

will stop in your gift shop is not specific enough and provides no believable analytical detail. This is what market research is all about; also refer to Chapter 14.

- What is the size of the market for your product or service? How many potential customers do you feel you could reach? This is what is called *potential market penetration*. If you've developed a new "sweep the world" concept for disposable diapers, then your figures for the United States start with the number of American babies wearing diapers. You would also include figures on the growth of the market, which would be the numbers of babies anticipated to be born in future years.

- Market analysis is also key. A market analysis would show a growth curve—even a successful new product will penetrate the market slowly, and there will always be customer loyalty to previous brands, so you will need an expert to help you depict what you might reasonably predict your market penetration might be, including information on making certain you can get the product to the marketplace.

- Positioning. Are you there for the high-end customer, or are you offering a product designed for bargain hunters? The segment of the market you intend to go after initially is a very important part of this early plan. Most companies start and end their days selling to the same segment of market. However, when you see Kmart hiring Martha Stewart to design for them, this is an excellent example of a company trying to lure a slightly different group of people into its stores.

- You will also be able to show potential sales revenue. When you pull all your financial figures together, you'll have a unit cost figure, so potential sales revenue would be figured by subtracting product cost from product income.

- To learn more about an industry, a particular company, or a group of target customers, check these Web sites:

  — *www.dnb.com*: Dun and Bradstreet; access to Dun and Bradstreet information on the Web.

  — *www.fuld.com*: Fuld and Company, a competitive intelligence company, is a site where you can find information about what else is going on in your field. If you think you're the first to offer something, don't be too sure until you've checked a source such as this one.

  — *www.thomasregister.com*: This site offers a particularly easy way to learn about markets and competitors.

- At the library, a librarian can help you use Lexis/Nexis, Pro-Quest, or Dow Jones to do more market research.

4. **Competition.** Understanding your competition is vital to business success. This is relatively easy if you're opening a Chinese restaurant. Between the telephone directory and word of mouth, you can quickly develop a list of other Chinese restaurants. But don't be fooled. These aren't your only competitors—you're actu-

ally competing with all other restaurants in the area. When families choose to go out for a meal they may opt for Chinese food, Mexican, or traditional diner food. If you know that a particular community has a love affair with its Vietnamese restaurant, then even superior food with a different ethnic twist is not guaranteed to get them to switch.

If you're starting a Web site, a mail order company, or a consulting business, listing your competitors becomes even more difficult, but you've got to do the best you can. The way you position the company will help narrow the field. The pricey skin-care spa in Westport, Connecticut, will attract a different clientele than your back-to-nature spa that is more moderately priced. To find your competition, you need to locate those that are serving the customer you intend to attract.

5. **Marketing Strategy.** How do you intend to get customers? This section should list:

- Major print advertising plans.

- Use of radio/TV.

- How the Web can be used to broaden your marketing.

- Ideas for publicity campaigns.

- Yellow Page listings.

- Special onsite promotions.

See Chapter 14 for additional marketing strategies.

6. **Operations.** This section describes the actual running of the business. If you have not yet addressed your physical facility—whether it's a factory or your home office—do so in this section.

   If you intend to sell fresh flowers daily, where will those flowers come from, how will you keep them fresh, what will happen if your first-choice source dries up? A dress manufacturer would need to walk through the process of obtaining the fabrics necessary for manufacture, as well as who will do the design, pattern making, cutting, sewing, and packing, and on what type of a schedule.

   A complex business may have many elements to its operation. You needn't describe any one aspect in detail, but you will want to make it clear that you have ways to overcome bad weather, delays in receiving your raw materials, a strike by the shipping service you use, etc., so that commerce can go on. This is also excellent mental exercise. By anticipating problems and working them out, you'll be better prepared to cope with them.

7. **Your Management Team.** This may be you or several people, but in this part of the plan you'll want to describe who is running the company and why they are particularly well-qualified to do so.

   Your background and credibility are key to the functioning of your business. Both a resumé and a personal financial statement should be added. They can be placed with other miscellaneous items in the appendix, but be certain to make reference to them here.

8. **Finances.** Later in the book, you will learn to put together an income statement, a balance sheet, and a cash-flow analysis. For the purpose of your business plan, you will need to prepare a projected (pro forma, as it is called) balance sheet, including sales, cost of operation, and profits on both a monthly and annual basis (see Chapter 9).

   You will need to specify the cash required for operating the business; most people should figure out what they will need for three to six months of operation. Also provide information on how you have funded the business thus far, such as from savings, loans from friends, or a bank loan. If you have received a loan, specify for how much as well as how and when the loan must be paid back.

   Investors and banks are not going to be interested in handing over a sum of money unless they have a general idea of how it's going to be used. If you're hoping to borrow $20,000 for specialized equipment, indicate that, along with information on how you plan to repay the loan.

   While all of this is necessary for obtaining funding, it is also very important in putting together an annual plan because it provides you with the same guidance a budget does for a family, so be sure to work carefully through the steps in Chapter 9. It's an important part of the process.

9. **Appendixes and Supplementary Items.** This section would include any documentation of your financial projections, as well as any of

the product information: a brochure, photographs, or press release you may have written—anything that heightens someone's understanding of the business.

If you work in a field that uses technical terminology, also provide a glossary. Those who read your plan will want to have a way to understand what you've written.

WHAT AN INVESTOR OR BANKER LOOKS FOR

When someone is considering putting up money to support a business, he or she is primarily watching for three things:
- Management skills and the ability to run this particular business.
- Repayment ability.
- The value of liquified assets in the event of default.

THE FINAL COPY

At this point, go back and write your summary of the plan you've just prepared, and outline the subjects covered so that you have a table of contents.

If you intend to use your plan to try to entice investors, remember that a good plan is just like a first interview—it needs to make a good impression. Write and rewrite it. Show it to your mentors, spell check and proofread it, and make certain it looks first rate. Use color photographs of products (or at least color photocopies), and put the entire project in a good-looking binding of some type. If it's truly a great business idea, then it deserves to be given the time to spiff it up so that it's just right.

KEEP IT SIMPLE

1. Even if you don't intend to seek investors, the smart business owner will prepare a business plan anyway.

2. Research each step of the process carefully so that you'll have an accurate blueprint from which to work once you're open for business.

3. If you get bad news during the planning stage (business won't be profitable, too much competition, etc.), consider yourself saved. You can still start your own business, but you've been spared starting one that is doomed to fail.

3

THE LEGAL ASPECTS

OF RUNNING YOUR OWN BUSINESS

WHAT'S AHEAD

Three Types of Legal Structures
Fifty-Fifty?
Limited Liability Company
Keep in Mind
Consider These Options Carefully
Things You Should Know
The Use of Experts

Whether you're selling handmade jewelry from your home, running an exercise studio, or aspiring to build a multimillion-dollar Web site, you'll want to consider the various legal structures available and set up the form of business that will offer you the right type of protection. Whether it's someone tripping on your living room carpet on the way in to view the jewelry or a partner in the Internet company trying to finagle his way out of a deal, appropriate paperwork can make all the difference in protecting what is yours.

THREE TYPES OF LEGAL STRUCTURES

While you'll need local experts to help you set up whatever form of business you choose, here is a brief outline of the various structures:

Sole Proprietorship

The majority of small businesses in the U.S. are sole proprietorships. In this business structure, you and the business are operating as one. With a sole proprietorship:

- The only legal work required is whatever licenses or permissions are necessary for running your business. Contact your local county or city clerk's office to determine what is required in order to operate a business in your area.

- If your business involves sale of a product or a service in other states, you may need to obtain a federal license or permit. Contact the Department of Commerce in Washington, D.C., for information on obtaining a license for interstate commerce.

- Income earned is treated as personal income (Schedule C, Profit and Loss from a Business or Profession, with your standard 1040 Federal Individual Income tax return). However, you will also be required to fill out quarterly estimated income tax. Call the IRS and ask for the paperwork needed for submitting your quarterly tax payments.

- Sole proprietors may have employees. (As an employer you will need an employer identification number. Call the IRS office in your state for information.) Remember that you are legally exposed if a customer takes issue with an employee's actions. You'll want legal advice on any protection you should have.

- The primary disadvantage to a sole proprietorship is that all the legal and financial obligations are passed directly to the owner. The structure also does not provide for many options if you should need to raise capital.

- If you have a sole proprietorship and want to call your business anything other than your own name, then you'll need to file a d/b/a (doing business as) form, usually with the county clerk's office. A search through municipal or county records will reveal whether or not the name is available within the jurisdiction, and by filing, you'll now have the exclusive right to use the name within the area. (See the next chapter for complete information about naming your business.)

Partnership

A partnership is like a sole proprietorship owned by two or more people. If you're going into business with someone else, you absolutely must put together a partnership agreement. As the law stands, you are liable for any commitments your partner makes and vice versa, so a written agreement that outlines your arrangement is very important in protecting both sides.

If, for example, you've agreed to run the restaurant if your partner finances it, then you need to think through all the ramifications in case something goes wrong on either side. Or you may be in a partnership where you both intend to work as equal partners—but what happens when your partner decides to loan his brother some money out of the business?

A good bookstore will carry books on putting together a partnership, or you can consult some of the offices of volunteer experts listed in Chapter 4. Discuss the major points and draft them yourself. It will save you money when it's time to turn it over to an attorney, which you must do to make certain that all the necessary issues are covered and that the agreement is executed legally.

Depending on the percentage of ownership (it isn't always fifty-fifty), each partner would own that portion of the company's profits, assets, and debts (see box on p. 42).

Forming a partnership to have someone to help with the work or the financing is wonderful in theory; in actual practice, you need someone who complements your workstyle and with whom you feel you will get along. While partnerships are easy to create, they are difficult to dissolve. If you get stuck in negotiating the written agreement and disagree about responsibilities, the focus of the company, or some other issue, consider that it's better to learn early that something isn't going to work out. Walk away.

Keep in mind that in a partnership one partner can make a commitment by which all must abide. Will you be comfortable with whatever commitments your partner makes? The partnership is, by its very nature, unstable—you are never fully assured that your partner agrees with you, will go along with your wishes, or won't walk out on you. Because investors and bankers are well aware of some of the inherent difficulties involved in creating a partnership, they are sometimes reluctant to bankroll businesses that have chosen this type of legal structure. On the other hand, a good partnership doubles the skills available to you and increases the number of friends or relatives who may be willing to help you out with loans.

- If you do arrange a partnership, here are some of the ticklish issues to address in your Articles of Partnership:
  — Percentage ownership and responsibilities (including the amount of time to be invested by each);
  — Prohibition of outside business activities that would compete;

— Whose decision prevails in case of a dispute;

— Who signs the checks and who has access to the bank account;

— Salaries to be paid to each partner and whether or not these salaries are to be treated as expenses in determining distributable profits.

- Spell out how the partnership can be ended. Can one partner buy out the other? If so, how will a price be set?

- A limited partnership provides certain partners with a maximum financial liability equal to their investment. It consists of at least one general partner and at least one limited partner. The general partner takes responsibility for running the business; the limited partner puts up the financial backing. A limited partnership must be run according to very specific laws, or it may be construed by the courts to be a general partnership, making everyone liable.

FIFTY-FIFTY?

Should you divide your company fifty-fifty? Only if you must. Unless the two of you have been in the yoke as equal contributors since the idea was born, try to retain a level of control. Fifty-one/forty-nine doesn't hurt the other person much, and it still gives you control.

Forming a Corporation

Corporations are legal entities created through the state where the business is incorporated. Upon forming a corporation, you can then issue shares of stock to shareholders, who become the owners of the corporation. You may receive financing, expertise, or product from the shareholders in exchange for the shares of stock you give them.

A primary advantage of incorporating is the ability to sell shares of stock in order to raise capital. The downside to this, of course, is that you now must answer to the demands of shareholders. If Uncle Benny invests with you because he thinks you'll turn a profit in three years, you may be doing some explaining if you're not at the stage he hoped you'd be when he wants to sell his shares back to you.

Sometimes the business owner is the only shareholder and board member. While this gets rid of the "Uncle Benny" problem, it creates another:

One of the primary reasons people incorporate is for liability protection. A corporation is liable for its own financial and civil liabilities. The shareholders risk only the amount of money they have invested. However, if you maintain sole ownership of all the stock, the corporation may be viewed as an extension of the individual. In addition to this, because you are just starting out, you may need to personally guarantee the obligations of the company in order to obtain credit or get loans. In this case, one of the main benefits of incorporating is taken away—that of limited liability.

However, if you intend to build the type of company where you want to be able to sell stock in that company, then incorporating is a good decision.

- By incorporating, you are creating a legal entity that can live on whether or not you remain involved.

- The amount of paperwork required annually for a corporation means that there is additional expense involved initially, as well as on an annual basis because you will almost certainly require professional help.

- The benefits of limiting your liability (and keeping your home and bank account safe) must be weighed against the amount of paperwork involved in starting and maintaining a corporation.

- There is a risk of facing double taxation (through the corporation and then through your personal income statement) when you incorporate. However, a good accountant can help you evaluate what type of income you can expect and how you can structure the corporation so you don't have to pay twice.

- If you're seriously considering incorporating, check out some of the books available on this topic alone, and seek out local professional advice. You'll need legal help to do it properly, and there are sometimes benefits in incorporating in another state. Get advice from a local attorney who can help you evaluate your type of business and what incorporating will do for you.

- To save on legal fees, obtain the needed forms from the secretary of state's office in your state. Fill them out and then review them with an attorney. The actual filing process you can do on your own.

- You'll also need to visit your bank to fill out special forms for setting up a corporate account. The bank will require that you spell out how the company will repay any loans that are due, and what assets can be seized if the repayment is not made.

- Most new businesses that incorporate will be forming a privately held corporation. This means that shares are held by a few people, often family members who also sit on the board and participate as officers of the corporation. The shares are not available to the public. (If more than 35 people become shareholders, you will be subject to regulation by the Securities and Exchange Commission, or you may choose to form a limited liability company, or LLC.)

LIMITED LIABILITY COMPANY

A limited liability company (LLC) is a relatively new form of business that provides personal liability protection the way corporations do, and still provides tax profits at the individual level only as S corporations do. There are fewer restrictions placed on LLCs as to the number of shareholders and their nationality, and this form of business is anticipated to become very popular for start-ups.

KEEP IN MIND

- Up until the late 1990s, those starting Internet companies were eager to "go public" and make their shares available to the public. Who wouldn't be, when initial offerings started at $10 or $12 (meaning that this is the capitalization the company is looking for through sale of the stock) and the stock skyrockets to $120 to $150 within a few days? Taking a company public requires careful thought and planning, because once you sell shares on the open market, you become beholden to a whole new set of bosses—your shareholders.

- On an ongoing basis, corporations must hold shareholders and board of directors meetings, provide minutes of these meetings, hold elections, advise shareholders of changes in stock disbursements, and file corporate taxes as well as filing quarterly estimated tax payments.

- An S corporation is another option. You incorporate normally but file an additional form 2553 with the IRS to establish your S corporation tax status. With this structure, corporate income is passed directly to the shareholders and declared as personal income. S corporations retain all the legal protection provided by a standard corporation (known as a C corporation). This decision needs to be based on projected income, and you'll want to talk to an accountant and an attorney beforehand. What can be a tax advantage at one level may be a tax penalty if your company makes more than anticipated. Get advice.

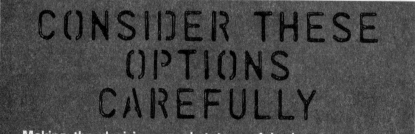

CONSIDER THESE OPTIONS CAREFULLY

Making the decision on what type of business structure to choose is not easy. Get advice from people who can help you evaluate the type of business as well as your options on various structures. In general, a sole proprietorship is good for a reasonably risk-free business that is primarily dependent on one individual. If you're a graphic artist and don't intend to have staff, then a sole proprietorship is perfect for you. If you find the business growing and you decide to add more artists, you can incorporate later.

The person starting a house painting business is in a different category. There are risks: one of your painters might drop a bucket of paint on the homeowner's toe, or that very painter may hurt himself getting down from a ladder. And if you're the boss, not the painter, you are creating a business that could go on without you—it may be worth incorporating.

Tread carefully when it comes to partnerships. Sometimes people are eager to do something "with a friend," or they take on a silent partner because they need cash, and ultimately, they live to regret it. After much thought, you may still feel a partnership is appropriate. Just be sure to spell out clearly how the partnership can be dissolved.

THINGS YOU SHOULD KNOW

- No matter what type of entity you choose to form, you must still check with your local government about business-related regulations that apply to your business. The psychiatrist seeing patients at home, as well as the coffee shop accepting 4 A.M. deliveries in midtown, may both be subject to local zoning laws or fire regulations. Call your county clerk to learn more.

- If you plan to operate in more than one state, you need to file forms in each state where you do business. Ask your attorney about this paperwork; there are law firms that specialize in this. (The name you intend to use must be available in all states where you plan to operate, so before creating stationery and brochures, be sure you'll have permission to use the name on which you're setting your sights. See the next chapter for more information.)

THE USE OF EXPERTS

The process of starting a business is an expensive one. You may be wondering, "But why do I have to hire someone for all this? Can't I just figure it out?" Not really. That old saying about the time to use a lawyer is before you need one is quite true.

Take the time to find the *right* professional. Your brother-in-law may be a prosecutor, but that doesn't mean he's the right attorney to help set up your business. Business law requires a special expertise, and you're better off with someone who does this professionally. Get referrals from other business owners. If you plan to do business in more than one state, be sure that the attorney is qualified to practice, and understands or researches the laws of that state. That said, there are steps to take to help minimize your costs:

- There are entire books dedicated to the legal aspects of running your start-up—do your homework on this and any other issue that is concerning you. This way you know what questions you want to ask when you sit down with a professional.

- Make a list of questions for your meetings. You won't waste time and leave feeling like you didn't get everything covered.

- Turn to your professional for expertise, not legwork. Say that you are watching your money and ask that the attorney have you perform any legwork, leaving the professional work to him or her.

- If your professional thinks you've got a hot idea, he or she may be willing to barter services for stock (or a percentage).

KEEP IT SIMPLE

1. Learn about the various legal structures for setting up your business, and consider the advantages and disadvantages of each.

2. Consult an attorney who can help you assess the situation with your business in mind.

3. Hiring expert help is well worth the money, but you can reduce costs by doing some of the legwork and filling out some of the forms yourself. Then let the expert review them.

4
NAMING YOUR BUSINESS

AND TAKING CARE
OF OTHER DETAILS

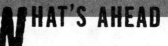

WHAT'S AHEAD

Choosing a Name
Other Details
Reckoning with Taxes
Insurance
Getting the Advice You Need

Once you've resolved the legal issues of starting your business, there are still a good number of business details to take care of. One of the next ones is fun—choosing a name for your company.

I'll never forget trying to help one of my friends think of a name for her new cosmetics company. She wanted something glamorous, catchy, memorable, elegant, uncommon—the perfect name. We agonized over short names, long names, descriptive names, abbreviated names. We made lists, bounced the ideas off other people, and thought endlessly about it. As the days dragged on, she began thinking that naming her business was anything but fun! Finally, she decided to proceed using her own name—a fine choice to begin with. How do I know? Today it's a name known throughout the entire U.S.

CHOOSING A NAME

The best company names are those that customers will easily remember and associate with your business. There are two steps to finding the right name. The first involves selecting one that you like; the second involves obtaining the legal right to use it. As you go through this process, consider:

- Names that are thought to be easily forgotten by consumers include geographic terms and personal names. Eastern Ice Cream (because you're in the eastern part of town) or Steve's Grill has nothing that helps a consumer remember it, yet with some effort, you certainly could create an unforgettable connection between the name and your business—it just may take a little more work.

- Many people want to use their own name as part of their business. Unless you are already well-known (and local fame is good enough if you are starting a local business), then you'll have to work at "branding" your product or service under your own name. There is nothing to connect "Audrey Smith" with her accounting services until she becomes known for the work she does. Developing yourself as a "brand" is entirely possible. It's a method that has worked for me. While I certainly could have worked with some type of "organizing" company name, I wanted to market my own knowledge and services rather than send out a team of consultants to represent me.

- Pleasantly clever names or names that describe the business are often successful. The company Bed Bath & Beyond successfully describes exactly what merchandise is available, and the name is easy to remember. Lean Cuisine not only helps sell the product, but because it's rather fun to say, it's more memorable. Eskimo ice cream bars and Poland Spring bottled water bring up appropriate images for their products. Similarly, a restaurant called Mom's Home Cooking would conjure up a better image than Steve's Home Cooking.

- The West Avenue Jewelry Shop has its benefits if you are 100 percent sure you will never need to move from the premises you plan to rent or buy, but should you need to relocate to a street besides West Avenue, then the name becomes very confusing.

- If you're starting a service business, ask opinions about the names you're considering. You may find that people think McGrath, Beekman and Smith sounds like a law firm, not an interior design company.

- Once you've selected a name you like, you need to conduct a search to be certain it's available for use:

  1. If you plan to incorporate, check with your state's secretary of state to see whether your proposed name is the same as or too close to any existing corporate names in the state. If it is, you'll need to turn to one of your next-choice names.

  2. If you're not intending to incorporate, then check with your county clerk to see if your proposed name is already on the list of assumed names used in your county. (Very few states maintain a statewide list of these names, and in this case, your county clerk may tell you to check the state level as well.)

  3. Conduct your own "confusion" search. Check telephone directories for the areas in which you plan to do business, and scan through the Yellow Pages. Though there may be no direct match to the company name you want to use, there may be a powerhouse business in your field that has a similar name. If

you proceed with the name you're considering, you may find that customers confuse you with a competitor.

- Depending on the type of business you're starting, your county clerk or the secretary of state will have the necessary forms to fill out.

- Even if the name is clear for using as a business name, if you hope to use it as a name that identifies your product, you may still have a problem with a service mark or trademark violation. For example, even if no one is using the name Ford Toy Store, you could anger the Ford Motor Company if you tried to market your own line of products. While you might get away with Ford dolls, you would run into major difficulty with Ford toy cars. To clear your chosen name for this type of use, you'll need to conduct a trademark search. Ask your attorney about this. You can also refer to *www.uspto.gov* for patent and trademark office information.

- If you intend to use your business name as a trademark or service mark, you'll need to file an application with the U.S. Patent and Trademark Office to reserve the name for your use and protect it by doing the following:

  — Capitalize the first letter.

  — State on your packaging or advertising that the mark belongs to your company.

  — If you've registered it, use an R with a circle around it to indicate this.

- If you've registered the mark only within your state or not at all, use the letters TM for trademark or SM for service mark to indicate your ownership.

- Enforce your rights by notifying other businesses and the media if they're improperly using your mark.

- Take care of all these issues now in order to avoid costly trouble (having to change your company name) in the future.

OTHER DETAILS

- If you plan to sell products, you'll need to contact your state's consumer protection agency or contact the Federal Trade Commission, Sixth and Pennsylvania Avenue, N.W., Washington, DC 20580, 202-326-2222 or *www.ftc.gov/*. The information provided will guide you regarding laws that cover such things as advertising, pricing, door-to-door sales, written and implied warranties, and, in some states, refund policies. While the hallmark of a good business is a strong customer service policy, the rules outlined by the government will provide you with a base from which you can work.

- If you plan to run any type of food-related business, contact the county health department. The kitchen used will likely require some type of approval, and there may be a regular review process.

RECKONING WITH TAXES

Taxes are as much a part of your business life as they are a part of your personal life—perhaps even more so. Meet with your accountant to find out what taxes you'll be paying.

- Though you should still obtain the advice of a professional, you may do some of this tax "homework" on your own by visiting the Internal Revenue Service Web site. Click on "publications," and review what is available online to be downloaded or read onscreen. There are many helpful publications for the small business owner.

- Set up records to keep track of everything right from the beginning. This will be a real time-saver.

- If you're an independent contractor, you will probably have to pay your taxes quarterly. There are specific rules about how much money you must have earned to be able to file a quarterly versus a yearly tax return, so you'll want to get up-to-date information on this.

- If you'll be collecting sales tax, work with your accountant on record keeping and timing of payments. If you do business in more than one state, you may want to assign this task to your accountant—it could be a nightmare.

- Expect to feel the pinch on FICA (Social Security) and Medicare taxes because you will be paying both the company share and the employee's contribution as well.

- Double taxation occurs occasionally when a business pays taxes on its annual profits and then you personally are taxed again when it comes to you as personal income. Work with your accountant on ways to avoid this happening to your hard-earned dollars.

- Other helpful Web sites include Taxweb (*www.taxweb.com*) and Sales Tax Institute (*www.salestaxinstitute.com*).

INSURANCE

- Contact your insurance agent and explain to him or her about your business. Keep in mind a few of these points:

  — *Home business* Eventually you may have quite a sizable investment in equipment and supplies, and these things will not be automatically covered by your homeowner's policy.

  — *Outside office space* Just as you would in your home, document your business possessions, including equipment, office furniture, and store display items. Save your receipts and take photographs or create a videotape that documents what you have. Store the documentation in a safe deposit box so that it is off the premises.

- Also ask about:
  - *Property insurance* for protection against losses from physical damage and theft.
  - *Business liability insurance*, which protects you if an employee or customer is hurt on your premises as well as if you drop a law book on a client's foot while visiting his offices.
- Other types of insurance you may need:
  - *Professional liability insurance* Doctors, lawyers, and a few other types of consultants may require a higher level of liability insurance to protect them against suits based on alleged professional error.
  - *Product liability insurance* may be needed to protect you against lawsuits arising from the use of one of your products.
- If you have employees you will need workers' compensation coverage.
- If you use your car for business, ask about obtaining an endorsement or a separate policy (what you need depends on your state laws).
- If you sell products on consignment, tell your insurance agent. You want to make sure your business insurance policy covers you for loss of "personal property of others" left in your possession.

GETTING THE ADVICE YOU NEED

Starting your own business is confusing because there are so many details to take care of. Whenever you're becoming concerned, look for guidance. There are people out there with business experience of their own who are willing to help you:

- SCORE (Service Corps of Retired Executives) is an arm of the Small Business Administration. Retired businesspeople donate their time locally to help guide those starting out. Check your phone directory or call the SBA for the phone number of the SCORE office near you. They'll try to pair you with someone who has run a similar type of operation or has experience that will expand your knowledge.

- Small Business Development Centers are collaborative programs put together by the SBA and local colleges and universities. They also provide free counseling. Call 202-205-6766 to find an office near you.

- Minority Business Development Centers offer low-cost assistance to women and minorities who want to start a business.

- Local and industry resources. You may find the guidance you need through people you know. Industry meetings and organizations like the Rotary Clubs and your local Chamber of Commerce offer opportunities to meet other businesspeople. The retiring architect you meet may be delighted to take a look at your business plan and share some of the ins and outs of starting your own architectural design firm—he might even refer some clients to you. Or the person you meet at the Kiwanis lunch may run a business that sells a different product to the market you're targeting. Talking to people you know can be an ideal way to get advice.

KEEP IT SIMPLE

1. Select a company name you like and then do the proper searches to be certain it's available for use. While this is time-consuming (and it will cost money to register the name) the inconvenience of starting a business and having to change the name midstream would be far worse.

2. Thoroughly investigate what you need to know about taxes before starting your business. Good record keeping from day one will make all the difference in helping your business run smoothly.

3. Check into your insurance needs, and be certain you are properly covered.

PART TWO

THE

PHYSICAL

SETUP

5

LOCATION, LOCATION, LOCATION

WHAT'S AHEAD

Home Is Where the Business Is?
Thumbs-Up for the Home Office
Staying Within the Law
Opting for Commercial Office Space
Buyer Beware!
The Retail Establishment

"**L**ocation, location, location" is a phrase often used to describe what should be top priority when buying real estate. When it comes to starting your own business, location is also a major decision. While it might be nice to get a luxurious corner office in a downtown commercial building, or to open a store on the best-traveled corner in the retail area, most start-up enterprises can't afford it. And even if you could "make rent" this month, you don't want to be burdened with an ongoing expense that is too high, becoming "house poor," in homeowner terms.

This chapter will first address location for the business owner who needs office space. Keep reading if you have hopes of being a retailer where foot traffic considerations are a primary issue.

HOME IS WHERE THE BUSINESS IS?

If you're considering running a business from home, there are both advantages and disadvantages. On the positive side:

- The price is right, and establishing a home office makes part of your home and related expenses deductible.

- It's comfortable and convenient.

- For parents it offers a possible solution to some child-care issues (it poses others as well, as we'll discuss). If your children are of school age, then you can work while they are in school but still be at home when they are, eliminating child-care costs.

- With some types of businesses, your clients never come to your office so there is no need to have space to "show off."

But running a business from home isn't always a perfect solution:

- It requires great self-discipline to work from home. It is sometimes hard to control the home interruptions and distractions so that you can work.

- The kids may actually find it confusing to have a parent there but unavailable to them.

- Your work is always there. Those who work from home may find it difficult to draw the line between family and work time if work becomes all-encompassing.

- Some businesses should never be run out of the home. If you have a good number of employees, receive deliveries via large trucks, generate foot traffic that would mean people parking on your street, or conduct any other type of business that might be disruptive or unsafe for your neighbors, then you need to base your operation in a location that is properly zoned for business activities. Even if you are a social worker or psychiatrist whose patients could park in the driveway you should think carefully about whether or not you want people coming to your home.

- If you decide to be home-based but have an occasional client who comes to your office, you need an accessible office (not an upstairs back bedroom) or a well-kept den or living room where you can meet with them. An ideal arrangement is a room that is accessible by a separate entrance.

THUMBS-UP FOR THE HOME OFFICE

If you decide that working from home is the right decision for now, here are some of the things you'll need to consider:

- When selecting the space for your home office:
  — If you have children, select space where you are away from the primary family traffic pattern.

  — If clients will come to see you regularly, select space where you can meet with them without having to bring them through the entire household in order to reach your office.

  — If you have a product, think about where you can store inventory and perform the packing and shipping necessary. Though your office may be on the main floor, you might decide to section off an area of the basement for storage and shipping and receiving.

  — If you need space for an employee, do you have it near your own work area?

- In order to qualify for a tax deduction, the space you select must be used exclusively for business.

STAYING WITHIN THE LAW

- The legalities of operating a business from home vary from community to community, so your first call should be to your city or county clerk. Even if you have no clients, customers, or special deliveries coming to the home, it's important that you know by what laws you are governed. You want to be more knowledgeable than your neighbor if he or she should ever complain.

- The issues that concern communities include:

  — Traffic—both customers and deliveries. Neighbors frown on the block being parked up or on having a semitrailer truck arriving to deliver shipping boxes to your home.

  — Employees. With extra people there will be extra street usage and additional cars.

  — Outside signage advertising your business. This is generally not permitted in a residential community.

  — Waste, excessive smells (such as from a catering business), and noise are all issues that will create difficulties with the neighbors.

- In some communities you will be expected to get a special permit or license. The county or city clerk will have this information.

Opting for Commercial Office Space

If your business is too big or too obtrusive to operate from home, you may want to lease commercial office space. Like good retail space, you will pay for location. Prices will be higher for space in a new centrally located building with a spacious parking lot than prices for office space on a side street with no dedicated space for parking. You'll need to evaluate how important both presentation and convenience are for you and your customers.

- Spend a day with a realtor who is willing to show you the market. Only after comparing locations in various parts of town and various amenities (elevators, windows, reception desk, security, etc.) will you be able to set your priorities.

- Think through your use of space. Will you need space for a receptionist? How many offices do you need? Do you require a conference room? (Some buildings have extra space that can be used occasionally.)

- While you want to rent enough space so that you have some room to grow, you don't want to take on so much debt that a business downturn for a couple of months sends you into a panic.

- Consider your commute. When you work for someone you have no control over the length of your commute. This time you have total control, so make certain it is reasonable.

- Consider parking. Is there adequate parking for customers? If customer parking is scarce, you don't want your car or that of an employee's taking up space for customers, so ask where you and staff members can park. Sometimes a landlord will have an arrangement with a parking lot in the area, and it can be used for staff parking.

- In some communities, being near public transportation is more important than parking.

- Check out the other tenants in the building and next door. Are they compatible with your business? If you're starting a day-care center, you don't want to be located above or directly next door to businesses that may need a peaceful environment. If the kids are enjoying themselves, you don't want to be worrying about whether they are making too much noise.

- Check with the other tenants about building upkeep and their feelings about the landlord. If at the end of your two-year lease he's going to demand a huge rent increase, it's better to be warned of this now. Or if he's skimpy with the heat during the winter, this, too, would be helpful to know in advance.

- Also ask about typical utility bills.

- Has the building gone through the necessary ADA (American Disabilities Act) compliance? Even dance studios need to be accessible and have accessible bathrooms. If the realtor or landlord is assuring you it isn't necessary, check this out with your local buildings department yourself.

- If the neighborhood is not the best, drive through it at various times of the day. Call the local police precinct and ask about the crime rate.

- If low cost is more important than location right now, ask your realtor if there are any tax incentives or other benefits to taking a less prestigious location.

- You may find that convenient, low-cost, and utilitarian may be as good as chic.

BUYER BEWARE!

Before signing the lease, you have to verify that you will have permission to run your business in that location. Some surprising issues can come up: Malls frequently have rules about how many of a certain type of store can be operated within the mall. (Ten sneaker stores wouldn't make for very interesting shopping.) And communities may restrict the whereabouts of certain types of establishments. You will not be permitted to run a commercial business in a residential area, nor will your manufacturing company be allowed to operate in a retail area; you'll need to locate in the part of town zoned for industrial use. Each town decides upon its own set of zoning rules, so you need to learn what applies locally. Some limit the number of takeout restaurants on a busy street, or if town parking is scant, a community board may require that you provide a certain number of parking spaces for customers before you receive permission from the town to open your business.

THE RETAIL ESTABLISHMENT

For the retail business or retail food establishment, location is key. In most cases, you need to be easy to see and easy to reach in order to be successful. (A Hollywood-style restaurant in a remote location where its remoteness becomes part of the appeal may do well, but this type of business is the exception.)

Unfortunately, locations with good traffic are also the most expensive in the area. If you're worried about the cost of the corner location you'd really like, think about these alternatives:

- What about a very small shop on the best street? Retail success is measured in sales per square foot, and while a large space may feel roomy, it's hard to keep your square-foot sales high. In a small location with creative displays, using walls and floor and ceiling, you may be able to run a very profitable business in very little space.

- Consider a location "around the corner." Would the town permit a sandwich-board ad on the main street to help draw customers around the corner for your goods? In one community, a new sandwich shop rented space just off a main avenue, and soon became known among patrons as the "secret sandwich shop" (though the business has a different name). In this case, its slightly-off-the-beaten-track location has become part of its charm.

- If you can't afford the highest-traffic area, look around your town for another interesting retail neighborhood. If you're running a jewelry shop, is there anywhere else in town with a cluster of shops that appeal to your potential customer? Renting space in that location might be less expensive and very good for your business.

- Check with other store owners in the immediate area you're considering. You may learn some interesting facts that will make a difference in where you decide to rent.

KEEP IT SIMPLE

1. As nice as it would be to set up an office in a luxurious commercial building, don't overspend on your rent. You're going to need a lot of money for running your business.

2. At first, consider working from home. You can move out when your income merits it.

3. If you need commercial space, don't sign anything until you're guaranteed that you can make any changes you need to, and read the lease carefully.

6

SETTING UP YOUR OFFICE

WHAT'S AHEAD

Planning Out New Space
Other Considerations
Avoid Employee Feather Ruffling
Setting Up a Home Office
Office Space Prep List
Furniture
Equipment
Other Items You May Need

In addition to the practical aspect of providing you with an efficient place to work, your office setup affects how people feel about you—and how you'll feel about yourself. I've visited some "high-profile" companies with glamorous public images, yet once inside visitors are confronted with overcrowded offices laid out in a grid-like fashion, packing in way too many employees. It felt unimpressive and out of character for what these companies stand for. (What's more, I can rarely find my way around these rabbit warrens!)

Once you've selected space in a commercial building or chosen to use space at home, you now need to turn it into a working environment that suits your needs and one that is in harmony with your overall company image.

PLANNING OUT NEW SPACE

If you're working with raw space, then you have several choices to make. First, think through:

- How many people will require space?

- Do you need a reception area?

- What type of floor plan meets your needs? There are three basic choices:

- An open floor plan where everyone has space within one large room.

- Private offices for everyone.

- Partitions between desks to offer some semblance of privacy.

- Consider your business and your employees, and what kind of environment might work best. An Internet start-up employing a bunch of twenty-something-year-olds might thrive with the open floor plan that encourages a collaborative workstyle. A legal office where privacy is important to the employees may do best with partitions or private offices.

- Now pretend you are a client or customer. Open the main office door and envision the layout you are considering. Will it be welcoming to outsiders? If not, what can you do to make it more pleasant? An open office layout that might look like mass confusion to a visitor can be hidden behind some type of attractive partition, for example.

- Some offices work with a combination of different designs.

- Whatever you choose, be certain you have the landlord's approval for any work that needs to be done.

OTHER CONSIDERATIONS

- Do you have products that need to be packaged and shipped? If so, you will need to plan for a shipping area.

- Does your business involve any hazardous materials (chemicals for photo developing, special cleaning products, etc.)? You'll need to check the laws in your state regarding the handling of such materials, and abide by them. In addition, you'll want to make certain you have a safe place for using and storing them. If the product is used inside, there should also be ample ventilation.

- Where will you put any equipment? (Keep noisy equipment out of earshot.)

- Have the wiring checked by a qualified electrician. In an older building, you may need to update the capacity or at least add outlets. Adding extension cords or "octopus" adapters is hazardous.

- Think through where telephone and Internet hookups should be placed.

AVOID EMPLOYEE FEATHER RUFFLING

Anyone who has ever worked in a major company knows the significance attached to office allotment. We all know who gets the corner office with the windows. . . . To get your company off to a good start, you'll want to be mindful of the pecking order.

- Take into consideration the use of "work groups." Who should be placed together in order to work more effectively?

- Now consider rank. Within each of those groups, assign the senior-most person to what would be considered the most desirable spot. You may even want to stipulate the area where you're placing the department and then let the "department head" help decide who goes where.

- Specify what decorating and additional touches are permissible for employees. Asking someone to remove an oversize plant or a wall of family pictures is poor for company spirit, so decide ahead of time what you will allow.

SETTING UP A HOME OFFICE

A similar evaluation needs to take place if you plan to work from home. You'll need to arrange space for yourself as well as any employees, keeping in mind some of the points discussed in the previous chapter regarding the best area of the home for the office.

When basing your office at home, keep in mind that not everything related to your business must go in the same area. Your shipping area could be in the basement, or your photo processing closet could be located separately from your main work area. For the IRS you need a square-footage figure, not a specific location such as "my den" when taking the home office deduction.

- Bring in a high-speed Internet line. No business should be without it.

- Review your phone lines and needs. You must have separate lines for home and office, or you will find that you could be receiving business calls at any time of the day or night. Otherwise, consider the number of office lines you need, keeping in mind your requirements for a fax line and possibly an Internet line, if your community is not yet wired for high-speed access.

- If clients will come to you, make the area they will see as professional looking as possible.

- For complete information on creating a well-organized, practical home office, refer to our book *Organize Your Home Office!*

OFFICE SPACE PREP LIST

Here's a checkoff list to use when setting up your office in either your home or a commercial building:

If construction work is needed:

_____ Consult an architect for ideas/plans if major work is planned.

_____ Heating or AC work needed?

_____ Painting?

_____ Check with landlord for approval.

_____ Find contractor/carpenter/painter.

_____ Get building permit for work to be done, if needed.

General prep

_____ Unless the building is new, bring in an electrician for an evaluation of the wiring and the equipment you plan to run.

_____ Have additional outlets added if needed.

_____ Add carpet or have existing cleaned.

_____ Get office cleaned.

_____ Consider signage. You may need anything from lettering on your door to an awning or billboard outside your office. Exterior signage sometimes must be approved by a community board, so before investing any money, ask your landlord or call the town clerk to ask if special approval is necessary.

- Go through the following lists of items you'll need, and make the appropriate purchases. Then take the time to organize your office so that you're ready to do business.

FURNITURE

Setting up an office is costly, and you'll want to minimize your expenses where you can:

- Spend money on the items that affect your well-being. Top-notch office chairs and desks at the right height for you and any employees should be your top priority in this category.

- Don't be too thrifty when it comes to the functional items. A good file cabinet with easy-to-slide drawers is money well spent. A cabinet that tips or one where the drawers stick will quickly seem like a tremendous waste of what money you did spend.

- Good lights are worth the investment. An old lamp from a tag sale could have faulty wiring.

- When it comes to a visitor's chair, a front desk, or any other sort of office furniture, save where you can. Secondhand chic, acceptable pieces from your home, or new furniture from one of the furniture superstores that feature good prices may fulfill your needs.

- Auction houses and office liquidators can be good sources for lightly used affordable furniture.

- Don't overinvest! You need your money for running the business. If you put too much money into what are nonessentials, you could find yourself owing a large sum of money just for setting up the office. You can upgrade later on.

- Purchase what you need from this list:

  _____ Bookcases
  _____ Computer table(s)
  _____ Conference table and chairs
  _____ Credenza
  _____ Desk(s)
  _____ Desk chair(s)
  _____ Files
  _____ Lamp(s)
  _____ Storage cabinet
  _____ Wastebaskets

EQUIPMENT

- When it comes to buying your equipment, the computer system should be your first priority. Computers outdate themselves relatively quickly, so don't buy used or "make do" with an old one from home. Purchase a new system that features speed and disk space so that you get started with the best system possible.

- **Find out how to set up the system so that the system is backed up regularly, and then do so. Experts say that it isn't a question of whether a computer will crash, it's only a question of "when."** You need to set up a system that protects you. Losing data pertaining to your new business could cause your business to crash as well.

- For a large piece of equipment such as a copier, consider buying a used one. Any sales organization that sells copiers will likely have some refurbished ones available, or they may offer convenient terms on leasing an office machine. On either, as well as on a new one, pay for the service agreement. Service and parts are big expenses. Even if the machine is only cleaned a couple of times each year (and cleanings are necessary to keep a machine in good working order), most service agreements are worth the investment.

- A cellular phone isn't exactly "office" equipment, but it does seem to be vital to doing business today. Some people are using their cell phones for all their telephone needs. Though this is not a long-term solution for a growing business, it is a short-term alternative. Select a good cell phone that has built-in voice mail and offers the promise of Internet access.

- Similarly, laptops are becoming required items. Some computer systems offer desk systems with a detachable laptop, or you may decide to invest in a separate laptop computer to use when you're on the road.

- At the very least you'll need:

  _____ Answering machine (if your system doesn't have voice mail)

  _____ Computer and printer

  _____ Fax machine

  _____ Telephone system

- In all likelihood, you'll also want:

  _____ Copier

  _____ Postage machine

  _____ Scanner

OTHER ITEMS YOU MAY NEED

To complete your shopping for needed items, consider which of the following you'll need:

_____ Bulletin board
_____ Business letterhead
_____ Computer disks
_____ Computer/fax paper
_____ Note or message pads
_____ Pens, pencils, highlighters
_____ Printer cartridges
_____ Software programs:

_____

_____

_____

_____ Staplers, scissors, glue, paper clips

Miscellaneous

_____ Bathroom and cleaning supplies
_____ Coatrack
_____ Coffeemaker and cups
_____ Office decorations (Keep this affordable.)
_____ Small refrigerator (This may seem like an extravagance, but if you can bring your lunch some days, it will save money in the long run.)

KEEP IT SIMPLE

1. Whether you're leasing commercial space or working from home, think through your use of the space. Plan it out and then make certain it makes sense by walking through it as if you were a visitor.

2. Spend money on the items that will make you work more efficiently—a good computer system, for example—and be comfortable in the process, i.e. buy a good desk and chair.

3. Purchase the supplies you will need and organize them so that once you are open for business you can function easily.

7

YOUR CYBER LOCATION

AND HOW BEST TO USE IT

WHAT'S AHEAD

Naming Your Site
Creating an Effective Web Site
Creating Great Content
Working with Search Engines
How to Attract More Customers
Maintain Your Pages
Use the Internet for Savings and Profit

aving a Web site is becoming as much a part of running a business as having a business card. Many business start-ups are mounting Web sites to use as digital brochures: "If you'd like to know more about my business, just check my Web site . . ."; a good number are using their sites as a way to capture names of potential customers, and still more small businesses are selling products or services via the Web.

In addition to the benefits of having a Web site, you will find that the Internet is one of the best business tools a business start-up ever had. It allows you to increase your contact with customers and potential customers, provides savings through price comparisons that would have been unmanageable in pre-Internet days, and offers amazing opportunities to enhance your business' sales.

NAMING YOUR SITE

- Determine your domain name. Using your company name for your domain is ideal, but sometimes your first-choice name is taken. (More names have opened up now that the registries are listing sites with other than .com suffixes, and this change will continue to expand your possibilities.)

- The site name should be one that is clear and easy to remember. If you have to—or decide to—pick a name that is different from your company name, select a title that describes your business. If you sell educational toys, you might work with titles like "smart toys" or "smart kids."

- Avoid anything too general. If you sell lighting with an emphasis on antique pieces, then get "antique" or "vintage" into your title rather than using "lighting" or "illumination." This will bring to your site customers who are looking for specialty lighting, not the college kid looking for a light for his dorm.

- Run a careful check of the validity of the domain name you would like to use. Search the availability of it by checking *www.internic.net/*. Check as carefully as you would check trademarks, trade names, service marks, and service names. You'll soon be spending major investment money on advertising and promotion, and you want to proceed with a name that you know will be rightfully yours.

- If you have a name you like but aren't quite ready to put up a site, pay a small fee to register your name with *NameSecure.com* or *NetworkSolutions.com*, and they'll hold the name for you.

CREATING AN EFFECTIVE WEB SITE

- The first step in creating an effective Web site is deciding on its purpose and how you would like it to look. Take a week or two to think about what your primary message is.

  — Is this site an electronic brochure, or is it a site from which you will solicit leads or sell products?

  — What can you offer that will draw customers to your Web site, and what might bring them back again? A baking catalog that is now online as well as distributed by mail has a Web site that features cooking tips and recipes, providing value for potential customers who visit. The promise of new recipes should bring customers back again and again.

  — Visit the Web sites of similar businesses and decide what you like and what you don't like about their sites. Evaluate content as well as Web design. Check out my Web site, *www.reisenberg.com*, and that of other business owners you know. The more sites you see, the better prepared you'll be to plan out your own.

- Write out a Web content plan. Before investing time electronically, you need to write out exactly what your content is going to be. Group your information logically, and make a map of how your visitors should progress as they move from page to page.

- Create each page so that it can stand alone. Since people like to bookmark pages, each visitor may have different favorites. Each page should have a clear, self-explanatory header. "Services offered by XYZ Company" or "Electronic Products offered by XYZ Company." Be sure to have company contact information, and a navigation bar. Some experts also recommend that you place a copyright notice on each page.

- Keep pages short.

- Make notes as to design elements you'd like to include.

- Use full names and information on each page in case someone has arrived at your site indirectly (e.g., a friend gave them a link to a specific page, not to your main page).

- Have a link to your home page on each page so that someone who came indirectly can find out more about who you are.

- Put your snail mail address and phone number on your Web site. People often want to talk to a human, stop by your store, or contact you in some way other than by e-mail.

- The temptation to capture the names of potential customers makes the idea of adding a registry form very tempting. However, if people have to spend a long time entering basic information about themselves before they can enter your site, you'll cut down on your number of visitors. Put registration information later in your site, and offer benefits. Why would someone want to hear from you again? Or why would it be helpful for them to leave their name on your site? Think this through carefully. Some registration programs make a visitor start all over again if they fail to enter a single piece of data or if they make a mistake. (Nothing is more annoying for a motivated visitor than being asked to start over!) Be sure your registry captures what they enter and then asks only that the visitor fill in the blanks.

- Once you have an idea as to the content of your site and how you would like it to look, you're ready to start creating the site itself. You have three options:

    — Hire a Web site designer to help you. Ask other business owners for recommendations and then check out the sites the designer has built.

    — Do it yourself using the many software programs available to people who want to create their own look. Ask friends or software store personnel for recommendations as to programs that are easy to use. There are also Web sites that offer tools for Web building.

    — Take a class on Web site design. These are available through many continuing education programs. This may be the perfect combination—you get to design the site yourself but you can benefit from the expertise of the teacher.

- Don't be overly ambitious in the beginning. You can always spiff things up as you learn more about Web design and what your visitors are seeking.

- Test your site and have others test it before putting it on the Web. Otherwise you'll lose your first customers.

- Now you're ready to put your site on the Internet. Contact your Internet Service Provider (ISP) and ask if they host Web sites. If not, you'll need to find a company who will host your site, for which you'll pay a monthly fee.

- If you plan to sell merchandise over the Web, you may want to put your Web site up on one of the hosting services that offer store building or shopping cart benefits. These sites offer merchant status, access to credit card acceptance and approval systems, and logs your traffic. While you still have to arrange an Internet connection through a normal ISP, for a small monthly fee these hosting services provide lots of solutions to e-commerce problems.

CREATING GREAT CONTENT

- Your first page should clearly state who you are and what you're selling (if anything).

- Keep it simple. Short chunks of information are the most readable, so keep your topic focused and write clearly and to the point.

- Make the site easy to use. People don't want to guess about what symbol to click on, nor do they want to go through too many screens to learn what they came to find out.

- If you want or need to provide more detail on a topic, create the site so that someone who wants to know more can click deeper into the site. Then those who want to zip right through to find what they are looking for can still move quickly; others can take their time absorbing what interests them. Most experts recommend that a visitor should have to click no more than four times in order to find any additional information they are looking for.

- Simple backgrounds with black type are the most easily read. A good Web designer may be able to create something slightly more elaborate for you, but resist going overboard.

- An elaborate Web site takes too long to load, and people won't wait. Oversize photographs and flashing graphics tend to be the elements that slow a site down. Keep your site simple enough that visitors with slower connections and slower machines can still visit you and find what they need without wasting a lot of "loading" time. The most important part of your site is that it should be accessible to as many people as possible.

WORKING WITH SEARCH ENGINES

- Register with several different search engines, and be sure you are listed with the major ones—Yahoo!, Excite, AltaVista, Netscape, and AOL: they bring in 99 percent of the audience. Go to each Web site and fill out the appropriate forms. There are companies that will register for you, but experts say it's best to do it yourself.

- Search engines find your site via your keywords. Therefore, it's important that your words be in your title, used early in the Web site itself, and repeated frequently. Simple keywords will work better with most search engines.

- Don't use the keywords over and over, hoping to get picked up more readily. Search engines cross off sites where the words are overused. Keep everything in context.

- Create metatags. These are the words you give a search engine that describe your site. For a Web page selling restaurant linens, the metatag might include "restaurant linens, table cloths, and napkins."

- Test whether your site comes up in a search. Go to Yahoo! or Excite and type in your keywords to see if your site pops up in the top thirty or so. If not, rethink some of your site.

- If your site does not come up early during a search, investigate which sites do. Then see what they are doing differently from what you are.

- Link with partners. Search engines give higher ranking to sites that link elsewhere. Work with others who target the same customers and cross reference to each other. You can exchange links and possibly share e-mail lists.

- Resubmit to your search engines when you make significant changes to your Web site.

- Investigate helpful software. There are "Web positioning" programs that submit your site to certain search engines and monitor your standing on the charts; some even keep a log of your visitors.

- Don't depend solely on search engines for bringing in traffic. The top sites promoted by search engines are those that get the most hits and have the most links, so any method you can use to bring people to your site is worth trying. (See box.)

- To learn more about search engines and how best to work with them, visit *www.searchenginewatch.com*.

HOW TO ATTRACT MORE CUSTOMERS

- Use traditional media to promote your site.
- Put your URL (Web address) on your business cards and fliers and include it in all your advertising.
- Promote your Web site the way you promote your business. Create a buzz by thinking of fun things to offer through the site. Offer product discounts and coupons, or even sponsor a contest.
- Answer all e-mail that comes in via your Web site. It's important to have high standards of customer service. (If your response is overwhelming, there are software programs that will send somewhat personalized answers out for you. They base their responses on keywords of the writer.)

MAINTAIN YOUR PAGES

- Start a "what's new" page so that you have a place to add information, and where regular visitors will have a quick way to learn the latest information.

- Check your links regularly and be certain they work. Just as you don't want a broken door blocking people from coming into your retail store, you want to be sure the path for Internet visitors is easy to use.

- Check your logs to learn more about how your site is used.

- Invite customer comment. The feedback you get may provide you with important information on how your site can create better value for the customer.

- Keep browsing the Internet to get ideas you can use for your site.

USING THE INTERNET FOR SAVINGS AND PROFIT

The Internet is an amazing tool for the small business owner. There are innumerable ways it can be of service to you. Here are just a few:

- Use the Internet to find help. If you search the Web, you're likely to find the exact type of help you need. Need a brochure printed? E-mail your written copy to an online graphics/printing company, and they will do the work for you. Need a presentation assembled? E-mail your materials to a company who will oversee getting everything done for you. With a company like Mimeo.com, you upload your copy to their printer, where the presentation is printed, bound, and delivered via overnight mail to you or to your client(s). What's more, the ease with which this can all be done now means that you print only what you need. Place your order and it will be printed and delivered on demand.

- If you have consultants, freelancers, or clients with whom you need to speak regularly, then consider an Intranet linking. Intranet linkings of individuals or companies who work together are of enormous help to businesses of all sizes, and it doesn't take a major expenditure for you to set up a link of your own. Currently a company called eGroups offers a free service that allows you to establish a central work area for a project team or other group that is working together. The benefits include:

  — The ability to send an e-mail to everyone involved in the project, which makes it easy for everyone to be up to date on what is happening.

  — Documents can be uploaded and stored in a work area. If several of you are working on a group presentation, the latest version can be made available and updated as people work on it.

  — A group calendar can be used to coordinate responsibilities. Automatic e-mail reminders can grow from the dates listed on the calendar.

  — Real-time private chat ability for team members. This is particularly valuable if you are collaborating with several people in different locations, and you would like to have regularly scheduled, virtual meetings.

  These systems are ideal for people who need a central management "office." It's a great way to manage a project or get the latest information out to salespeople, etc.

KEEP IT SIMPLE

1. Take time to visit lots of Web sites and plan out the content and the mapping of your Web site carefully.

2. Register with search engines but use other ways to tell potential customers about your site: list it in your sales literature, publicize it, and find creative ways to bring people to your Web site.

3. Maintain your site. Update it frequently and be certain that it's in good working order.

PART THREE

MONEY, MONEY, MONEY

8
FINDING MONEY

WHAT'S AHEAD

Assessing Your Business Needs
Sources of Start-Up Money
Savings
Family
Establish a Relationship with a Bank
A Bank Loan
The SBA
Incubator Money
Private Investors
A Corporate Partner?
Venture Capital
Online Investors

Some people keep hoping to find a "rich uncle" or to win a lottery in order to start the business of their dreams. If you really have a business you want to start, don't wait for a miracle source for funding. There are ways to get the money—you just need to investigate which one is right for you.

ASSESSING YOUR BUSINESS NEEDS

For most people, the initial thought of having enough money to start a business seems overwhelming—how could you possibly ever have enough to afford it? However, just as you would create a good family budget, you can do research followed by some very basic math, and you'll quickly learn how much money you need. Then you can begin to look around for ways to fund your business.

Begin by thinking through exactly what you will need to start your business:

- To begin, you need to make a projection of the size of your business starting out. If you're opening a gourmet takeout coffee shop, do you expect to have any sit-down tables? How many hours do you expect to be open? How much staffing will that require? What will you sell besides hot coffee and coffee beans? In order to assess how much money you'll need to run the business you have to develop enough of your plan to know what kind of expenses will be involved.

- Must you rent space? If so, visit a local realtor and get a general idea of how much you need to allow for this expense.

- Do the same with any equipment needs you have. Some businesses may need office equipment only. Other businesses will require very specific machinery. A carpet cleaning company will need special cleaning equipment as well as a specially designed truck to run the equipment. Call around and find out what it will cost to purchase or lease it.

- Make a list of office supplies, quantities, and prices, and do the same with any special supplies you'll need.

- Calculate what you'll need to invest in initial inventory.

- Must you hire staff? How many? What will your annual costs be?

- Will you be liable for any taxes, even before your first sale (property taxes, etc.)?

- Refer to the next chapter regarding putting together a financial statement.

- Take whatever time is necessary to assess what kind of funding you'll need to start your business.

- Be conservative. Carefully consider "worst-case" scenarios, such as a "down" month in consulting, or a slow start-up for a retail store. When you're starting a business there are always surprises.

- There are consultants who can help you come up with the figures you need. A retail expert will be able to tell you about how much you need to sell per square foot, how many customers you need daily, what the average sale should be per person in order to show a profit. The end result will be a start-up budget, how much capital you will need, and how long it will last. While you can certainly find these experts locally, you may also get help online. For custom research for market and operational figures, try *www.myliveassistant.com* or find a specialist through *www.EXP.com* or *www.ExpertCentral.com*.

SOURCES OF START-UP MONEY

To find the cash you need, there are several sources to consider. Each has its benefits and its drawbacks, and you must evaluate them based on what will be more comfortable for you.

SAVINGS

As discussed in Chapter 1, there are many reasons to keep your "day job" for a while once you decide you want to start a business. Even if you work in a job unrelated to the business you want to start, maintaining employment for a time gives you the opportunity to build up your savings account. You read about being certain you had enough money to fund your personal life during a start-up. The other piece of this is setting aside some money for your business—virtually all business start-ups are partially funded by personal savings.

FAMILY

Family members may be happy to help you work toward your dream, but if you decide to approach a relative about a loan, be very clear about the arrangements and very careful about the amount borrowed:

- Don't borrow money the other person is counting on for something else. If your mom needs the money to buy a new car in a year or if your brother offers to loan you some of the savings he's set aside for his preteen's future college education, don't accept the loan. The stress and worried comments from a person who might begin to second-guess loaning the money is not worth it. Find your funding elsewhere.

- If you have an uncle with "money to burn" who is happy to extend you a loan, iron out the details as seriously as if you were working with a bank. Draw up a loan agreement that states the amount of the loan and the interest due. The agreement should also outline a specific schedule for repaying the loan. Doing business with family can be tricky, but by putting an agreement in writing, you'll always be able to counter Uncle Steve's Thanksgiving comments of "You owe me money!" with "Hey, Uncle Steve, I know I do, but that next payment isn't due until January."

ESTABLISH A RELATIONSHIP WITH A BANK

Deciding where to set up your business banking account is more than just deciding what bank is most convenient to where your office will be located. You need to select a bank that is friendly to small businesses and offers terms that will be favorable to you for your finances.

- Set up an appointment to visit with a bank officer. You not only want information about the types of accounts available and their costs; you also want to know about the bank's attitude toward loans. Some are much more interested in loaning to small businesses than others.

- If you are lucky, your current bank, where your personal accounts are located, will be receptive to expanding your relationship, and the bank officer may try to offer you somewhat more favorable rates. This is helpful because if you should need a loan, a long track record with the bank can work in your favor.

A BANK LOAN

You may have built up equity in a home, and many people get home equity loans in order to get the start-up cash they need. These loans are relatively low-risk for the bank since they are secured by your home. Though you will need to state in the loan application that the money is for a business start-up, you won't undergo the grilling you might if you tried to take out a personal loan for the start-up. However, remember that this isn't "free" money. A home equity loan will add a new monthly payment to your expenses, so be sure to plan for this in your monthly budget.

While a bank will be most comfortable with a well-secured loan, such as a home equity loan, there are a few other options.

An unsecured line of credit. These are very difficult to get, but occasionally a bank will extend to someone—someone with a good net worth and an impeccable credit history—an unsecured personal line of credit. If you should get it, you can draw against it as needed.

A secured line of credit. These are somewhat easier to get. Banks will sometimes make a loan for the purchase of a specific asset, such as a piece of equipment or a building. The asset then secures the loan until it is paid back.

Short-term loans. Some businesses can get short-term loans using inventory as collateral (inventory is valued at no more than 50 percent of retail. If you defaulted on the loan, the bank would not get the full value out of your merchandise).

- When a bank considers you for a loan, they will be evaluating the following:

  — Who you are. Have you banked with them for a long time? Did you have a positive career history (and financial history) before you decided to start your own business?

  — Do you have the cash flow? If a loan is arranged, do you have money to cover the payments regularly?

  — Capital. What is the company's net worth?

  — The soundness of the venture. Have you successfully convinced them that you are running a good business?

  — Collateral. What would the bank get if you had to default?

THE SBA

Inquire about the Small Business Administration's (SBA's) loan program. Generally the SBA gets involved in the loan process as the "guarantor" of the loan, with the actual cash coming from a different source such as a local bank. This guarantee is designed to offer an incentive to commercial lenders so that they will increase the lending to small business. The borrower (you) must still meet the lending institution's requirements for collateral, experience, and the like. You pay interest to the SBA to repay them for their guarantee, and then you must pay principal and interest to the lender as well, per the specifications of the loan agreement.

Contact your local SBA office for a list of participating lenders in your area.

There is also some money available directly from the SBA, and it often goes to promising businesses that have been turned down by other lending institutions. However, the amount available for loan varies from year to year, and the process and paperwork can be cumbersome.

INCUBATOR MONEY

The National Business Incubation Association (NBIA) in Athens, Ohio, helps small businesses nationwide find low-cost space, management training, and financing. For a list of incubators in your state, send a self-addressed stamped envelope to the NBIA, 20 E. Circle Drive, #190, Athens, OH 45701, or visit their Web site at *www.nbia.org*.

PRIVATE INVESTORS

Some small businesses have successfully put together their own network of investors by asking for a smaller chunk of money from several sources. By putting together a strong letter and backing it up with a well-thought-out business plan, one business owner raised $50,000 by sending out 150 letters to people whom he knew and asking for only $5,000. Ten people responded to him, and with each, he worked out a plan for repaying the loan, which he so did, and on time.

A local business has a particular advantage with this type of loan structure because it gives your lenders a particular interest in seeing that you do well. Whether you're starting a restaurant, a flower store, or a gift shop, those who have put up some cash to help fund you should certainly support you themselves, as well as help out with building word of mouth.

A CORPORATE PARTNER?

If you have a business on which a larger business relies, you may be able to get some initial funding from your major customer, the corporation. For example, if you're starting a company that will provide Web design for a major client, you may be able to obtain funding from them and pay them back by reducing the fee for your services.

VENTURE CAPITAL

Throughout the country, there are forums that range from small investment groups to much larger ones, and their sole reason for being is to find business start-ups in which they want to invest. Most forums charge an application fee and offer brief one-day workshops geared toward helping selected candidates refine their presentations. The good news is the investors *want* to invest in people like you; the bad news is that because they see so many possible businesses, the investors are very experienced and may have seen a dozen other business proposals similar to yours. Consider them a long shot.

ONLINE INVESTORS

Some businesses are finding funding online. One resource is the Angel Capital Electronic Network (ACE-Net), *www.sba.gov/ADVO/ acenet.htm*, developed by a group of interested parties: the SBA's Office of Advocacy, the Securities and Exchange Commission, state securities regulators, and the North American Securities Administrators' Association. Qualified investors and entrepreneurs obtain passwords to have access to the Web site.

There are also other private sites that offer possible loans. Check out:

www.loanwise.com. Within five minutes of filing an online loan application, you will get an answer as to whether or not you will qualify for a loan from one of the financial institutions that participate in this site. The site also presents a selection of terms and rates so that you can judge what would be best for you.

www.ventureline.com. This site links investors and other funding sources with entrepreneurs.

There are many sites that favor Internet ventures and tech-based start-ups. Do a search and check links to see what you uncover.

KEEP IT SIMPLE

1. Determining the amount of money you need for your start-up is a painstaking effort but very necessary in establishing a well-funded new business.

2. Savings is certainly the best place to start when it comes to financing a new business. Many people also take out home equity loans, an available source of money that you may want to take advantage of.

3. If you're looking for major investors, you'll need to investigate venture capitalists, a corporate partner, or a way to interest personal investors. Just be careful what you borrow—and know exactly how you're going to pay it back.

9
YOUR FINANCIAL PICTURE

WHAT'S AHEAD

Preparing an Income Statement
Income Statement Worksheet
Preparing a Balance Sheet
Balance Sheet Worksheet
Doing a Cash Flow Analysis
Cash Flow Analysis Worksheet
Pro Forma Statements
Talk to Experts
Careful Record Keeping

A parent with a new baby takes her to the pediatrician for checkups and brags about height and weight gained during those early years. Parents also capture growth on videotape, audiotape, and on film—all in an effort to create a record for looking back to see how the baby has grown and changed. The same type of process needs to take place with your other "new baby," your business.

To document the health of your business as well as to capture how the business looks at a specific time, you don't need pediatricians or cameras. You need an accurate set of financial statements, so that you—or anyone to whom you present them, such as potential investors—can assess how your business is faring.

These documents are vital tools in the world of business. Not only are they helpful to anyone considering giving you a loan or investing in your business, but these records permit you to assess how your business is doing financially. If a downward cycle is indicated by one of your recent financial statements, you'll have time to modify your actions and improve the bottom line before the situation gets serious.

Even if you've always thought that financial statements were too complex to bother to understand, you need to start learning now. The material in this chapter is presented clearly, and you'll soon find that reading your own financial statements is actually quite fascinating. Combined, they offer a play-by-play analysis of how your business is doing: How is phone usage running month to month? What was the total cost of attending the out-of-town conference, and was it worth it? And then you can assess why widget sales in July were twice as good as they were in June. Did you have a particularly effective ad running? Did you try a special promotion?

Here's a rundown of the forms you need to understand. Try using this information and adding figures from your own business. What seems dry and boring when written out will suddenly come to life, because the financial information you add will begin to tell the tale of your own business.

PREPARING AN INCOME STATEMENT

An income statement, also called a profit and loss statement, is a summary of your financial situation over a given period of time. The key element of an income statement is that it covers income and expenses for a specific amount of time. *It doesn't deal with figures that occurred before the accounting period starts, and it doesn't continue beyond the end of the time period specified.* The fact that it covers a specific amount of time—and that time period only—is the main element that distinguishes it from the other types of financial statements we'll discuss.

The statement must record all revenues for the given period as well as your operating expenses. If you want to borrow money, an income statement is one of the financial documents you will be required to provide to banks or other lenders.

Income statements for most new businesses are done on what is called "cash-basis accounting." The money is accounted for at the time it comes in or is paid out. Sometimes, however, a lender will want to see a statement that has been figured on an "accrual basis." (Income and expenses for jobs are not factored in until after the final payment on a particular job is made. See Chapter 10 for a more detailed explanation.) Check with your accountant as to which method should be used for your income statement.

Elements of an Income Statement

Sales: Total revenue generated, less returns, and taking into account any discounts given.

Cost of goods sold: Even if you sold a thousand widgets at $10 each during a given time period, you did not make $10,000. On an income statement, you need to factor in how much each widget that you sold cost you: Let's suppose the cost of each widget was $4, and you sold a thousand widgets during this time period. Then your cost of goods sold is $4,000. You don't yet need to report the cost of any items still in inventory.

Gross profit: This is the cost of goods sold subtracted from the sales generated during the given time period. It does not yet include overhead operating expenses or taxes.

Operating Expenses for an Income Statement

This section of the statement includes the everyday expenses of running your business, everything from postage to promotion. Because every business is different, you will need to brainstorm all the categories in which your type of business spends money. Create a computer template for those expenses so that it will be easy to keep it up to date. A restaurant will have staffing and food supply expenses that a one-person Internet start-up won't have.

Possible expense categories include: advertising, depreciated cost of equipment such as copiers, computers, and fax machines (see "depreciation" in the next chapter), overhead (any expense that has to do with the general operation of the business that doesn't fall into other categories—insurance, office supplies, cleaning services, etc.), rent, salaries, sales-related costs (entertaining a client, travel to visit a client), and utilities.

Total Expenses

This is the sum total of all expenses incurred in running your business.

Net Income Before Taxes for the Specified Time Period

1. Subtract your operating expenses from your gross profit to arrive at this figure.

2. Now adjust this number by subtracting the taxes that are due based on this figure, and that gives you *net income*.

INCOME STATEMENT WORKSHEET

Company Name _____

    Time Period _____

Income

    Sales (revenue generated) _____

    Less cost of goods sold _____

    Gross profit _____

Operating Expenses

    Rent _____

    Overhead costs (utilities, janitorial, etc.) _____

    Equip. leasing or maintenance contracts _____

    Salaries _____

    Advertising and promotion _____

    Other sales-related costs, such as entertainment,
        travel, sales materials, etc. _____

    Office supplies _____

    Other: expenses unique to your business _____

    Total expenses _____

Pretax Profit	
(gross profit less expenses)	_____
Federal/State Taxes	
Pretax profit	_____
Net Income	
(profit remaining after taxes are subtracted)	_____

PREPARING A BALANCE SHEET

If you think of an income statement as a traffic report on your business, a record of what's come in and what has gone out during a specific period of time, then it might seem logical to think of a balance sheet as a still photograph. Your balance sheet provides a picture of your business' financial condition at a given moment in time. The building you inherited for your restaurant won't be reflected on an income statement; however, it is an important asset to be listed on a balance sheet.

The first part of a balance sheet is a listing of the assets of the business. These are items of value owned by your company.

Assets themselves are described as *liquid* or *current assets*, items that could quickly be converted into cash, and *fixed assets*, items that could be converted into cash but might take more time to do so.

In setting up your balance sheet, start with the following:

Assets

—Cash: bank accounts, money market funds, and investments;

—Accounts receivable: what other companies are supposed to pay you within 30 days;

—Inventory: finished goods as well as raw materials to be turned into merchandise;

—Financial payments received (such as a payback on a loan you made) that are due within a year;

—Fixed assets: land, buildings, machinery, office equipment. (In this category, all fixed assets except for any land you own are depreciated from year to year. See the explanation of "depreciation" in the next chapter.)

—Intangible assets: assets you can't touch or see but that have value, such as franchise rights or a patent.

—Other: accountants may place cash value of life insurance, long-term investment property, and other types of assets in this category.

Liquid assets and current assets should be added together to give you your final tabulation for the "assets" column of your balance sheet.

Liabilities

The liabilities portion of your balance sheet reflects the amounts you owe. This will include loans, outstanding bills, credit card debt, and taxes.

Liabilities are generally broken up into short-term liabilities (meaning accounts payable or current money you owe to suppliers, employees, credit card companies, the IRS, etc.) that are payable in less than a year, and long-term liabilities (your mortgage, major equipment loans, bank loans, and other long-term financial obligations) where the debt extends for longer than 12 months.

A new business may start out with a balance sheet that is out of balance—one where the liabilities are greater than the assets. A healthy balance sheet should show that assets are greater than liabilities. If this is the case, then you are going to subtract your total liabilities from your total assets in order to "balance" (or make equal) the asset and liability columns: $500,000 in assets minus $325,000 in total liabilities would leave you with $175,000 in *equity*, meaning the value in the business.

Equity may be broken down to reflect stock ownership by outsiders, and into a further category called "retained earnings." If the company is making money (refer to your income statement), then most business owners choose to reinvest some of the income into the business, and this becomes the retained earnings. This is an accrued sum that should build up year after year.

As you watch your balance sheet change over time, your goal is to increase assets relative to your liabilities so that the equity in your business will continue to grow. (If your business grows, your expenses may increase, and that's fine, so long as your income is growing as well.)

With a balance sheet, the two columns must be in balance.

BALANCE SHEET WORKSHEET

Company Name _____

Date _____

ASSETS		LIABILITIES AND EQUITY	
Current Assets		Current liability	
Cash	_____	Salaries	_____
Accts. rec.	_____	Monies due in	
Inventory	_____	less than one yr.	_____
Paymts. rec.	_____		
		Long-term liability	
Fixed Assets		Mortgage and	
Land	_____	long-term debt	_____
Bldgs.	_____		
Machinery	_____	Owner's equity	
Vehicles	_____	(Liabilities subtracted from	
Equip.	_____	assets give you the amount	
		of the owner's equity)	
Total	_____	Total	_____

DOING A CASH FLOW ANALYSIS

A cash flow analysis statement, which can also be thought of as a "sources and uses of cash" statement, provides invaluable information because it documents how you're doing at managing your business. It is much like an income statement, but it solves the good month/bad month problem because cash from previous months is reflected on it. For example, a gift store may do 50 percent of its business in November and December, and during that time the store may generate more than enough cash to keep it going 12 months per year. Yet if you were to look at income statements from July and August, you might see that the business is doing quite dismally during the summer months, and there would be no way of realizing that financial strength during other parts of the year could compensate for the summer business doldrums.

Remember that an income statement reflects only the activities of a particular time period and does not take into account anything carried over from a previous one. Only a cash flow analysis provides the business owner or a potential investor with the information he needs to understand the overall financial story of the business.

The cash flow statement also gives you an accurate way to judge how you're managing your business. If a bad February happens because a client has started paying his bills late and, therefore, you're not receiving income at the time expected, this tells you to focus on improving collection. You can also track your expense categories month to month to evaluate your various expenditures.

This accounting method also permits you to plan and prepare for bad times. If your income statements show that in your industry, summer is a weak business period, then you can stockpile cash to get you through this period as well as do what you can to stimulate sales during that time because you know what's coming. You may want to offer deeper discounts than usual, hold a special promotion, or send your staff out to street fairs to sell in different venues. The cash flow analysis permits you to analyze how you can divert income from other sources (another part of the business, some consulting work you do, etc.) or from other sales periods during the year to help cover costs during a bad time.

In essence, this statement tells you: "At the beginning of the period (whatever time period is being recorded), my business had 'x' dollars in cash, and at the end of that time period, I had 'y' dollars in cash." Because the statement reflects all income and outgoing payments, you can look back and see exactly where the money came from (the "source," which can range from your consulting fees to cash gained from selling a piece of business equipment) and where it went (how it was "used").

The cash flow analysis is also well suited for guiding the business start-up that is not yet producing income. If you're starting an Internet company and rich Uncle Al has staked you with half a million dollars, a cash flow statement will reflect that money ("In the beginning I had $500,000 . . ."), and the expenses taken against it will show what you're spending (and how much is left) as the business gets under way.

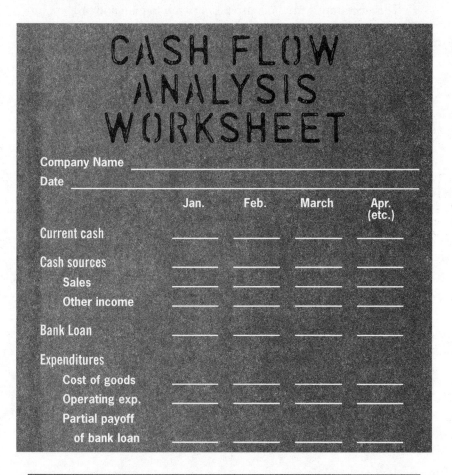

CASH FLOW ANALYSIS WORKSHEET

Company Name _____
Date _____

	Jan.	Feb.	March	Apr. (etc.)
Current cash	____	____	____	____
Cash sources	____	____	____	____
Sales	____	____	____	____
Other income	____	____	____	____
Bank Loan	____	____	____	____
Expenditures				
Cost of goods	____	____	____	____
Operating exp.	____	____	____	____
Partial payoff				
of bank loan	____	____	____	____

	Jan.	Feb.	March	Apr. (etc.)
Purchase of computer equip. and new office furniture	_____	_____	_____	_____
Taxes	_____	_____	_____	_____
Subtotal	_____	_____	_____	_____
(expenditures subtracted from cash sources)				
Ending cash	_____	_____	_____	_____

(If the subtotal figure is positive [you made money], then add that amount to current cash for your ending cash figure; if you lost money during the month, then subtract the subtotal from your current cash figure for your ending cash figure.)

During good months, your "ending cash" will be more than what you started with; during a weak month, your ending cash balance will be lower.

PRO FORMA STATEMENTS

Pro forma statements can be created for income statements, balance sheets, and cash flow analysis, and the purpose of these statements is to project into the future rather than analyze the past. These statements are created by working from your current income statement, balance sheet, and cash flow statement.

To create a "pro forma" statement of any one of these documents, you need to take each and work through how the figures might change over the coming year (or three years, depending on what it is you're projecting). In the process, they permit better business planning and help a business owner offset potential downturns in profitability.

For example, you may already know that your rent will increase by 5 percent for the following year, and you can anticipate that you'll need to add a staff member. In addition, your main supplier has indicated that prices will be going up on certain products by midyear. Take these numbers and put them into your pro forma statement, and you'll begin to fill in the figures you need for your financial projections.

The process is painstaking, but worth the effort. By working through what the future holds, you'll be well prepared to capitalize on any positive opportunities and offset any negative ones.

TALK TO EXPERTS

Talk to your accountant or seek help from some of the experienced professionals listed in Chapter 4. A good financial advisor or a person who is experienced in your field will be able to offer helpful guidance in putting together your financial statements, and what may have seemed like Greek a few months ago will begin to become your favorite map, a chart for where your business should go.

CAREFUL RECORD KEEPING

We've all gone to the bank and withdrawn spending money from the ATM. A few days later, we pull out our wallets and wonder where the money went. Money that isn't tracked (records kept as to how it is spent) just seems to "disappear."

In starting your own business, you can't afford to let money "disappear"; you must keep very careful records, or you will lose control of the business. Whether it's money received or money spent, write down the complete history of where your money is coming from and where it is going.

Careful record keeping is also necessary for the Internal Revenue Service. If you are audited, you will be extremely relieved if you have your financial records (and any documentation, such as receipts and canceled checks) up to date and in good order.

As the weeks and months go by, you'll find that you're creating a diagnostic tool that will permit you to adjust your business practices. You may see ways to increase income or ways to reduce costs. The end results will be the creation of the successful enterprise you've dreamed of.

KEEP IT SIMPLE

1. Every business owner—from the home-based consultant to someone doing an Internet start-up to the factory owner—needs to understand how to prepare and read financial statements. Within these documents lies the complete story of your business.

2. Take the time to prepare (or have prepared) pro forma statements that project into the future. Based on this information, you will be able to make plans for your business.

3. Hire an accountant. Whether you use him weekly or every now and then, you will find it invaluable to receive expert advice on your finances. Don't forget about getting advice from other business owners or business resources listed in Chapter 4. There is a lot to absorb, and the more you listen the more you'll learn.

10

KEEPING THE BOOKS

WHAT'S AHEAD

Start with Professional Help
Automate!
Evaluate Your Situation Monthly
The Simplicity of Cash
Offer Incentives
Extending Credit
Taking Credit Cards
Getting Paid
Purchasing
Bill Paying

133

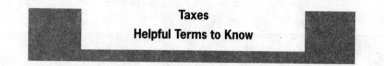

If you didn't excel in math while in school, you may feel you'll never be able to master the accounting end of your business, but don't despair. The financial part of your business really can be managed very simply. The key is to start off on the right foot with the correct type of software program for your business. You'll also want guidelines from your accountant as to what you need to keep track of and how to do so. If you keep up with the work involved, you'll find that it will never become overwhelming.

Here's Basic Business Finance Made Easy:

START WITH PROFESSIONAL HELP

Even if you've taken some accounting courses, talk to professionals to get guidelines for the particular type of business you're starting. As mentioned in the previous chapters, a good accountant can be invaluable to you, or you can contact some of the resources listed in Chapter 4 to find someone who can advise you in getting started.

If you want to save money and not pay for professional services right away, hire an accountant to help get you started. Then do most of the bookkeeping yourself; the new software programs today make it almost easy. That way an accountant is familiar with your business and can be available to answer questions, but you can hire him or her for the more difficult parts of the job, such as setting up your system and filing taxes.

An accountant is also the perfect person to help you figure out depreciation on business equipment, and he or she can be instrumental in making the process of filing taxes much easier.

You can also get more information online by visiting the Web site of the Internal Revenue Service (*www.irs.gov*). Take a look at publication #583, "Starting a Business and Keeping Records."

AUTOMATE!

In this day and age you must investigate the software programs that are helpful in your industry, and start using them immediately. While you may eventually delegate the work involved, it is important that you know enough about the program selected to use it well.

EVALUATE YOUR SITUATION MONTHLY

Just as you need to check your body weight occasionally, you also need to check the health of your business on a regular basis. Prepare an income statement each month (see Chapter 9), and also take a look at your balance sheet. This is easy to do with a good software program. By keeping careful tabs on expenses and income, you'll be able to catch a problem before it gets out of hand. These evaluations will also permit you to track trends. Are sales for one product increasing while the demand for other products is diminishing? It's important to be aware of what is happening.

If you do not take the time to track your business income and expenses, you will never be able to adjust in order to increase your profits.

THE SIMPLICITY OF CASH

The penny candy store had the right idea: Charge a small amount and expect everyone to pay you in cash. Then all you need to do at the end of the day is roll up the coins, count the bills, and stop by the bank.

It is the rare business today that can operate as an all-cash entity. Restaurants and retail outlets usually have to accept credit cards or checks. In business-to-business transactions, you almost always have to extend credit to other businesses and then wait to be paid. Internet companies are heavily dependent on credit cards; and even consultants who may get some payment upfront must generally wait until the end of a job to receive a final payment. Following is some advice on getting paid.

OFFER INCENTIVES

You need cash to run a business, so do everything you can to maintain a positive cash flow. Extending credit and making collections on money due you is so time-consuming (and so important) that it is worth offering a slight (1 to 5 percent) discount to any customer of any size who is willing to pay cash.

EXTENDING CREDIT

Whether or not you have to extend credit will largely depend on the type of business you run. The small kitchen shop does not need to maintain accounts for customers; the printing company or handbag manufacturer does.

- Establish what your credit policies will be before you start doing business. A first-time customer can be expected to pay in full on the first job. After that, you may need to be more lenient. What percentage of a sale must be paid as a deposit? What limit will you place on credit extended? Also, don't extend credit on orders under a certain amount. If you're just starting out, it's not worth your time to have to run around collecting small amounts of money.

- Set a "payment due" policy, such as payable in full within ten days of delivery. Check with others who run similar businesses, and then take a conservative approach.

- If a customer wants to place an order and expects you to extend credit, run a credit check on the customer right away. Prepare a form (or get one from your accountant) that provides you with banking information, as well as business references, and then take the time to check it out, paying particular attention to what the references say about on-time payment. As a new vendor, you will almost certainly be the last to be paid, so any hesitation about a potential customer on the part of the bank or the references should be considered a warning sign.

- If yours is a service business, you need to be just as professional about billings and collections as if you were selling dump trucks—maybe even more so. Once you've delivered a service, it's gone—you have little recourse if the client decides not to pay you. For that reason, your job proposals should specify payment in stages, with the final payment to be made "on final delivery of services."

TAKING CREDIT CARDS

Becoming authorized to take credit cards is a big hurdle for a small business. Until you can take credit cards, you're operating at a disadvantage as so many people expect to be able to say, "Charge it!"

Accepting credit cards increases the probability, speed, and size of customer purchases. Returns are also easier, so people feel more comfortable with using plastic.

To become eligible to accept major credit cards, your business must establish merchant status with a bank or online company representing each of the credit card companies you want to accept. (For this service, you usually pay the bank or online business a monthly fee as well as a per-transaction fee.) The process will take some time as companies are wary of approving new merchants, because if you go out of business and fail to deliver merchandise they are stuck absorbing the loss. Banks are also concerned about a product where there may be a lot of returns—crediting back money is costly.

- Contact a financial institution—a bank or an online provider—and ask for an application. Visa, MasterCard, American Express, and Discover require that you establish a merchant account through one of their "acquiring banks" in order to accept them.

- As a start-up, a mail order company, or a home-based business, you are considered high risk, so you may have to contact several banks before finding one who will accept an application from you. Start by contacting the bank where you have your business account, or shop around.

- Prepare to provide them with almost as much information you'd supply if you were taking out a loan. You will need to provide bank and trade references, estimate credit card volume, and speculate on what you would expect an average transaction to be.

If you can show good sales figures, it will help. If you make money, they make money, because you pay them a fee.

- If you are turned down by the first bank or two, ask other business owners how they have gotten credit card approval. Or look for an independent sales organization (ISO). For a fee, these businesses help you locate a bank who will grant you merchant status.

- Expect to pay certain fees connected with taking credit cards. There can be a start-up fee ($50 to $200), plus equipment costs for a card terminal, which can be a few hundred dollars, and a monthly statement fee as well as fees charged per transaction. Some of these fees are negotiable, but if you're just starting out, the odds of getting a "good deal" are very slim. In the beginning, you should just be happy you got approved.

- To maintain a good relationship with your bank or credit card company, you'll want to be very careful when checking credit cards. Always check the expiration date, look for a hologram or security mark, and check the signature of the person using the card. Then take time to get the sale authorized.

GETTING PAID

- Get very specific information from the customer about how and where to bill, including what information must be on the invoice (purchase order number? invoice number?) so that the bill will be paid promptly. Specifics on shipping should also be discussed. You don't want to give the customer any reason to give you a bad time.

- Set up a tickler system for invoices so that you can begin following up the moment the bill is due. When it comes to collection, "the squeaky wheel generally gets the grease."

- If payment is not forthcoming on a timely basis, you'll want to meet with your customer to discuss what he plans to do. A sincere effort to pay over an extended period of time is not optimum, but it is better than some of the alternatives, such as not being paid at all.

- Small claims court hears many cases of defaulting on payments. If the customer needs you and intends to stay in business, another option is to refuse to service the account until all bills are paid.

- Once you become involved in credit and collections, consult an attorney. Credit decisions and behavior during collection is regulated by law, and you need to be certain that you—or anyone working with you—carefully observes the regulations that apply.

(The laws primarily involve not denying credit based on race, sex, or ethnic origin; and the regulations on collection have to do with not harassing the person.)

- Credit collection companies will also track down money for you. Generally, their fee is a percentage of what they collect.

PURCHASING

Many people raised in the forties, fifties, and even sixties grew up in households where the family budget was carefully observed. Family vacations weren't taken until the money was saved, and an extra dinner out was a well-earned treat. To run your business well, you're going to run it in much the same way. (And you have your cash flow and income statements to help you.)

- Whether you're purchasing pencils or a backhoe, price shop.

- Get bids on major investments. Whether you're investing in a computer system or a copying machine, write out the requirements of the system (this is called your spec sheet), and let vendors bid on it. You'll also find this process educational—you'll learn many things about the items you're buying when listening to the salespeople. Absorb what is helpful.

- To the new business owner, a purchase order may seem like an additional hassle, but it's actually your best form of protection.

By writing out exactly what you purchased (size, color, any other specifications), you're protected from having to accept a "misunderstanding." One business owner learned this the hard way when ordering file cabinets. A major file manufacturer makes 36-inch lateral file cabinets in two heights—only half an inch different from each other. The business owner had carefully measured space for the cabinets, based on one size described by the salesperson. When the cabinets arrived and were half an inch taller than the ones the business owner thought she was purchasing, they were too big for the space allowed. The owner had nothing in writing, and an extra set of beautiful file cabinets now hold dead storage in her basement. *Putting everything in writing is your best protection against any future problems.*

- Rebid when you repurchase. In some business relationships, loyalty will be important; other times the cost will matter more.

- If employees do any purchasing for the company, set a dollar limit that they are not to exceed—you should have purchase approval over major purchases. Also stress to them the importance of watching the budget.

- When a product arrives, inspect it as carefully as your budget-conscious mom would a new carpet. Check the delivery slip to be certain that what was specified is what was received. Do this promptly so that any difficulties can be ironed out quickly.

BILL PAYING

Keeping track of who you've paid and how much is very important. It is not uncommon for a vendor to lose track of the fact that you've paid a bill, so always assume that the burden of proof may ultimately fall on you.

- Stay organized. File your bills carefully and pay them promptly. File your paid receipts by month or by category, and when your bank statements arrive, file these as well.

- Before paying any bill, read through the invoice to verify that you're being billed correctly and that the vendor is the one with whom you are familiar. Con artists sometimes send bogus invoices for office supplies that were never ordered or delivered, hoping that no one will check before paying them.

- Pay your bills according to agreement. A bad credit rating could bring your business to its knees.

TAXES

Once you start a business, you become liable for a host of new taxes. Meet with your accountant to help set up record books or software so that you can keep everything straight. Here are taxes that may apply to you:

- *Employment taxes:* Employment taxes are very complex, and unless you have only an employee or two, consider hiring a payroll service. (Your accountant's office may do this, or he can recommend a reputable service.) Not only must you pay taxes for your employees, but you are responsible for withholding some of what they owe as well. Any errors can cost you interest and can incur penalties. Get help. (Information from the IRS is available from 1-800-TAX-FORM.)

- *Sales tax:* Most businesses must charge some type of sales tax on what they sell. Some types of service businesses are exempt from this, and regular businesses who sell to tax-exempt institutions and to resellers, such as wholesalers and retailers, generally are exempt from collecting tax on those sales. Mail order sales to buyers in states other than where a company is based may not be subject to taxes. A hotly discussed topic is when and whether companies will eventually have to charge tax on sales made over the Internet. Check with your accountant. The requirements regarding taxes on mail order companies are already beginning to change.

- *Use taxes:* These are taxes on items a business may buy from out-of-state vendors.

- *Income taxes:* An incorporated business in the U.S. is liable for federal taxes, and usually state and local taxes as well. The tax laws for S corporations vary, so check with your accountant. Federal corporation tax returns are due on the fifteenth day of the third month after your fiscal year—if your fiscal year ends on April 30, then your taxes will be due July 15.

- *Estimated income taxes:* At the beginning of your second year in business, you will have to begin paying estimated taxes for the amount you anticipate earning in the coming year.

- *Property taxes:* Your company will be liable for real estate taxes on any real estate that you own, and in some leases, the renter is liable for taxes instead of the landlord.

- *Personal property taxes:* Some localities impose taxes on inventory, equipment, and furniture, among other things.

- *Other taxes:* Some states tax inventory held within their state; other areas charge taxes on lodging or on amusement facilities. You'll need to learn what applies to you.

Taxes are serious business, and good record keeping will be extremely helpful if the IRS ever asks any questions.

- Don't underreport income. A government audit can tie you up, cost you legal and accounting fees, and, if you've skirted the law, the IRS will win in the end. Be honest so that you can move forward in your business unencumbered.

- Use your accountant to prepare your taxes. The person taking care of your filing should be someone who knows the tax code well and can help you benefit where possible while still paying careful attention to the law.

- If the IRS asks questions, answer promptly and be as cooperative as you can. If they see that you're making an honest effort to explain something or correct a misunderstanding, this will work in your favor.

HELPFUL TERMS TO KNOW

- **Accounting Methods.** There are two common methods of accounting. The IRS requires businesses with inventory to keep records according to the accrual basis. If you don't maintain an inventory, then you and your accountant can opt for the one that works best for you.

    Accrual basis accounting: This method means that you don't credit income to the company until the job is complete or the sale is final, and the final payment is made. Expenses are also linked with a particular sale, and you hold expenses until they can be matched with the appropriate earned income. (If you had $350 in expenses on a $3,000 consulting job that spanned two months, you wouldn't record the income, $3,000, or the related expenses, $350, until payment was made, which could be four months from the time you actually started the job.)

Cash-basis accounting: This method counts sales and expenses when cash is actually received or spent, and income and expenses are never linked job for job. If you receive payment for an assignment in one month but the bills from that job don't come in for a couple of months, the records from this particular assignment will be in separate monthly accounting periods if you're using cash-basis accounting.

Though cash-basis accounting is simple, and good for businesses where the expenses and income occur in close proximity, most larger businesses use the accrual method because it provides a more accurate picture of how the business is doing.

- **Accounting Period.** During a specific accounting period, which can be a week, a month, a quarter, or a year, you compare income with expenses to evaluate how your business is performing. Most businesses evaluate performance at least four times per year, and you should do a cursory check each month to be certain nothing is glaringly wrong. This offers an opportunity to plan any changes that will improve your overall profitability.

- **Depreciation.** This is a way of accounting for an asset (a vehicle, a major piece of equipment, your office furniture, a building you own) to your business but taking into consideration that it loses value as it grows older. By taking the original cost of the item, say $6,000 for an office copier, divided by the number of years you expect the equipment to last (your accountant will give you a range, but let's say ten), you arrive at a figure that can be used for annual depreciation. By depreciating—and thus saving some on taxes—you can begin to build up cash for the time when you'll need to reinvest in a vehicle or a piece of equipment. (Land cannot be depreciated because it does not lose value.)

Because a balance sheet will call for reflecting "book value" of certain items, you will need to keep track of the rate at which you are depreciating something. For example, the "book value" of the above copier after only one year will be $5,400. ($6,000 divided by 10 equals $600, and then $6,000 minus $600 is $5,400.)

The above method is referred to as "straight line depreciation." Accountants often recommend ways of depreciating that permit you to accelerate the process. This may permit you to reduce tax bills earlier than with straight line depreciation, but you need an expert's advice to know how to go about this.

- **Expenses.** There are two categories of expenses:

  — Cost of sales: These are expenses directly connected with the cost of your product.

  — Operating expenses: Those expenses associated with running your company.

- **Fiscal Year.** Not all businesses work on a January through December year; however, a "calendar fiscal year" is the best way to begin. Later on, you and your accountant may decide there is reason to change it. A retail store is a perfect candidate for a change of fiscal year, because the busiest period is generally

December. A change to a fiscal year that ends in March, April, or May permits you to retain taxes due on income collected later in the year. Discuss your options with your accountant.

- **_Gross Profit._** This is the amount of money you make on an item after subtracting what you paid to acquire the item. A shawl that retails for $100 for which you paid $45 has a gross profit of $55 (out of which you then pay overhead, salaries, taxes, etc.).

- Review Chapter 9 if you want additional information about financial statements.

KEEP IT SIMPLE

1. Whether you are a neophyte or have taken some accounting courses, it's important to understand the financial side of your business, and it's equally important to seek expert advice. The issues can be quite complex, and you need intelligent guidance in steering your financial course.

2. Be careful in extending credit and watch your cash flow at all times.

3. Pay careful attention to all types of taxes—from payroll taxes to estimated income taxes. A professional can help guide you.

PART FOUR

BUSINESS SMARTS

11

KEEPING TRACK
OF BUSINESS

WHAT'S AHEAD

Being in business for yourself requires being organized—it is more important than you can even imagine.

You are taking on a big responsibility, and you'll frequently have to focus on more than one task at a time, be expected to make split-second decisions, and keep track of where you put what you need for today as well as what you're supposed to be doing tomorrow. As a result, you need to develop systems to keep track of your life, your contacts, and your paperwork.

Implement good systems from the very beginning. That way they will be in place when business picks up and you really need them. Don't "make do" with a small pocket calendar or a single file box for now because you're "not set up" or "not really that busy." Treat this venture like the business it is going to be, and invest in what you need so that you're functioning at peak productivity right from the start.

YOUR CALENDAR SYSTEM

Paper or computer? When it comes to calendars, that is the question of the day. Paper calendars are still a valid option, and my preference because I like their portability and the fact that I can jot down on-the-road notes to myself more easily than I can in a handheld computerized system. However, more and more people are opting for computer calendars and/or handheld computer calendars that "sync up" with their computer. A few others like the Internet scheduling programs. Here's what you need to know:

If You're Thinking of Paper

With a paper planner, look for a good-size one. You're going to be running a business based on what you write down here. (I also recommend that you keep track of personal obligations here, too. Trying to maintain two calendars is a guaranteed way to miss an appointment.) In addition, you'll want:

— Portability.

— Plenty of space for writing down appointments, as well as your daily "to do" list.

— An area for noting expenses and mileage—you'll need to create a record of all these things now that they will be deductible.

— Also evaluate the telephone directory. The telephone directory systems that are a part of computer calendar programs are first rate; with a paper-based system, you'll at least want accessibility and plenty of space for all the miscellaneous numbers people have now, ranging from cell phone numbers and beepers to fax numbers and numerous e-mail addresses. A good directory will have space for all this.

If You're Considering a Computer Calendar

If you're at your desk all day, you may be satisfied with a calendar program that runs only on your computer. You can always carry a one-page printout of your calendar if you need to. There are various models, many of which are created by the name-brand companies in the calendar industry. If you have a favorite paper calendar, ask for the computer version of it.

Some people like the scheduling programs that are available on the Internet. You can log on from any computer and go right to your calendar page on the Web. Compare the options offered on these sites with the features you like on the calendar you're currently using.

If You're Thinking of a Handheld Computer or Personal Digital Assistant

Today most people choosing to go electronic will be selecting handheld computers (personal digital assistants, or PDAs) that link with your desktop computer and permit you to work from either one.

- When selecting a PDA:
  - Be sure the screen is easy to read.
  - Evaluate size and weight.
  - Be certain that information is easy to enter. The ones where you have to use a stylus to enter stylized letters are a lot of trouble: however, if you like one of these models, a solution is to enter all data on your regular computer and then sync up to put it into the handheld portable model.

— Ask about backup. Those that link with your regular computer system are backed up every time you synchronize your system.

MUST-DO CALENDAR RULES

Once you've selected your system, I have three rules I recommend to clients and readers:

1. *Use only one calendar.* Though it may seem odd to be noting down soccer games and kids' dental appointments on the same calendar as your business appointments, it's the only way to keep track of your life. You're one person, and if your child is getting braces at 10 A.M. Monday and you've got to take him there, then you need to book your business appointments around that.

2. *Write everything down.* You may think that you'll "always remember" that you have a meeting with your accountant the first Monday of every month, but as your business becomes busier, it will become harder and harder to remember what now seems such an important part of your schedule.

3. *Look at your calendar every day.* You'd be surprised at the number of clients whom I see who simply forget to check their calendars!

CALENDAR TIPS

- Write down complete information when booking an appointment. Note name, address, and telephone number, and, if needed, directions to the office. This saves time on the day of the appointment, and with a computerized system, if the appointment is rescheduled, you can "drag and drop" the information so there is no rewriting.

- Write in appointments with yourself to block out time to get priority work done. This is particularly important for the small business owner because it is so easy to let your time get eaten up by nonessential tasks.

- Schedule telephone appointments for people who are hard to reach. By getting the call scheduled on both your calendars, you'll make it happen.

GETTING THINGS DONE: THE MASTER LIST/OFFICE NOTEBOOK

To manage a business, you need a way to keep track of the myriad details that will arise as you start your business. The solution is a Master List where you can write down *every*thing that you need to do. From this Master List, you'll cull the items that need to go on to each day's "to do" list, and it will make it possible for you to get everything done.

While many people like working from an electronic daily "to do" list, I recommend that you use a paper-based system—a notebook—for your Master List. Not only does it make a convenient way to record everything you think of at any time, but it provides a history of what you've accomplished as well. To get started using this system:

- Purchase a spiral notebook; lefthanded people may prefer a steno-style notebook. Spiral is better than looseleaf as this system works best if no new pages are added or removed.

- Create a running list of everything you think of—from "try calling Mr. Adams (a major potential client)" to "buy stamps." Include the telephone number and any other miscellaneous details you might need when you take care of the task.

- When you add a new entry, note the date just above your entry. This way you are creating a history of what you've done when; this can be helpful when looking back to check on anything from ordering printer cartridges to whether or not you've confirmed delivery arrangements for your next shipment of goods.

- Priority items should be marked with an asterisk or written in red.

- Big projects should be broken down into steps; set deadlines for each step so that you can get things completed on time.

- Cross off items as they are completed.

CREATING YOUR DAILY LIST

- At the end of each workday, set aside ten minutes to plan what you need to accomplish the following day.

- Examine the current day's "to do" list and carry over anything you still need to attend to. (If you work with an electronic list this will happen automatically.)

- After considering your next day's schedule and evaluating any out-of-office appointments, review your Master List and decide what additional tasks can be undertaken on the following day.

- Place an asterisk by those items on the list that need to take priority.

- Don't overschedule. Plan no more than 75 percent of your day. As an entrepreneur, you'll find that there will be many spontaneous items that will require your time, from a broken copy machine to a lengthy phone call with a potential client.

- Remember, if you overschedule, you'll become overloaded, worn down, and stressed out—the last thing you need to be productive.

CONTACT MANAGEMENT PROGRAMS

Contact management programs are software that automate the sales process. Virtually all businesses today could benefit from a systemized way to keep track of the people with whom they do business.

With contact management software, you can keep a complete record of customer addresses, telephone numbers, fax numbers, and e-mail addresses. In addition, you can keep track of when you last spoke with a customer, what you talked about, what his/her special needs are, and when you said you would call again. By keeping accurate records of this type of information, you have the opportunity to tailor your sales information to the customer's specific needs (based on information gathered over time), and with this personalization, your chance of making a sale increases.

Another advantage to having this information at your fingertips is that you're never caught off guard. If Mrs. Smith calls to ask just "one more question," you can type in her name, and her information will appear before you, permitting you to answer her more clearly and effectively.

A couple of major companies make contact management software, and the programs sell for less than $200. Ask friends for their recommendation or stop at a computer store and ask for a demonstration.

PAPER FILES

The ability to file so much electronically as well as the capability of pulling current data (like product or market research) off the Internet as needed is reducing our need for paper files. However, it is still important to maintain some paper files for legal and business matters as well as some types of customer information.

- Invest in a sturdy office file cabinet. "Designer" cabinets can be flimsy and fashionable systems like "basket" systems just won't stand the wear and tear of being used for a viable business. When making your selection, decide:

  — How many drawers of storage do you anticipate needing? If you currently store any documents, measure the space you have now and then try to estimate what your future needs might be.

  — Do you want four-drawer or two-drawer units? Four-drawer systems hold more but two-drawer ones can double as credenzas.

  — Based on your answers to the above questions, how many units do you need, and how many will fit into your office space?

  — Do you want to set up the drawers for legal or letter-size documents? (Most file cabinets can hold either.) Adjust the drawers for the appropriate size and then purchase suspension files as well as regular file folders that will fit.

— Create a color coding system to make it easier to find what you need. Green might be for insurance files, blue can represent client folders, yellow might hold all contracts, and red can be dedicated to suppliers.

• Once you've established a system, file regularly—preferably every night, but at least once a week. If you don't, those valuable papers you're looking for will reside permanently in your "to file" tray.

• Date what you file and note "expiration" times on anything you can toss after a certain date.

CTION FILES

No matter how much we are able to reduce our regular paper files by maintaining good computer files, I can't yet envision a day when "action/tickler files" won't come in handy. These are reminder files that hold all those miscellaneous bits of paper we just can't get rid of:

— Where do you put driving directions to a new client's office until it's time to visit there next week?

— How do you hold on to a hard copy of an agenda you received in the mail for a meeting being held in a month?

— And what about that mailing you received regarding a conference you may want to attend?

The answer is action (or tickler) files. To create this system, you need 43 file folders, one for each month of the year (12) and one for each day of the month (31) to be reused month to month. Select one color for the monthly folders and another for the daily. Label 12 for the months, and then write 1 to 31 on each of the folders.

Here's how the system works:

— The current day is May 1, and you are visiting a new client on May 10. In the folder labeled "10," place the driving directions you received along with anything else you need to be reminded of on that day.

— The agenda for the meeting in June should be filed in the "June" folder. When the date gets closer, slip the agenda into the date on which the meeting is scheduled.

— As for the conference you're considering attending next fall— put that information in the folder for the month when you need to decide. If the "early bird" registration ends on August 1, then you'll want to make your decision in July, if you can.

COMPUTER FILES

Once you start your own business, you'll soon feel that "your whole life" (and your whole business) is in your computer. For that reason, it's very important that you take the steps necessary to be certain that your data is protected from disaster:

- Use a surge protector.

- Use a well-respected antivirus program and update it regularly.

- Pay attention to virus alerts from friends and the media.

- If you accept a disk from anyone, run an antivirus scan before opening any files.

- Install a backup program.

  1. Make a complete back-up of your hard drive once a month. Save this copy until you make another full copy a month later. This copy should be kept somewhere other than in your office. Send it to your spouse's office or any place where you'd have access to it in case of fire.

  2. Make a full backup from week to week so that in case of a crash you have a reasonably up-to-date backup. (The monthly backup offers greater protection against viruses; if you were to have to rebuild your data, the older backup might be virus free even if the weekly backup isn't.)

3. On a nightly basis, copy onto a diskette anything you would hate to have to re-create if the computer went down in the next 24 hours.

4. In an emergency: If your computer is "acting up," and you're concerned you don't have time to back up properly, copy the files you're most concerned about and e-mail them to someone else or to another one of your computers. Later these files can be e-mailed back to you to be reinstalled into your machine.

- If you don't want to have to remember to back up regularly, investigate how to program your system so it does so automatically. Then you never have to think about it.

KEEP IT SIMPLE

1. Select a calendar system that is right for you, and then be sure to write *everything* down and check your schedule daily.

2. A good Master List of "to do" items is an ongoing list of everything you think of that needs to be done. Refer to this Master List every day to determine your daily "to do" list.

3. Use action/tickler files to keep track of miscellaneous items (invitations, directions, brochures, etc.) that pertain to upcoming events.

12

SMART TIME MANAGEMENT

WHAT'S AHEAD

Starting your own business means that more than any other time in your life, you will need to practice smart time management—different issues will demand your attention, and you'll need to become expert at evaluating what is most important to you and to the future of your business.

I recently was called in to consult with an interior designer who often works with people who are doing major remodeling on their homes.

"In my business, I need to stay one step ahead of my clients," she said. "But I find it so difficult—there are so many details in construction and decorating. I frequently get calls from my clients who seem to be one step ahead of *me!*"

When I asked about her client load, I got my answer to her problem. She was trying to provide personalized service to *nineteen* clients! Without a large staff that would be extremely difficult to manage.

Working with her I showed her how making her consultancy a little smaller would not only keep her sane but would help build business. Instead of miserable clients who felt like she wasn't doing the job, she instead had satisfied clients who were eager to refer her to others. The catch? The new clients had to pay more for her services! Soon she was making more money with less headache—the ideal business solution.

Smart time management is knowing how much you can do and still do it well. It's a fine balancing act, and one very much worth practicing.

STAY ORGANIZED

When it comes to organization, a new business has a big advantage over an old one: Because you are just starting out, you can establish and maintain an organized system for running your business. Be stern with yourself about this—a well-organized business will save you time. No hunting for a missing file, no wondering where you put last month's sales figures, and no worrying about what you did with that potential client's phone number. It's important to establish systems and maintain them.

TEN SYSTEMS FOR BETTER TIME MANAGEMENT

- Create a good calendar system and don't leave your office without it.
- Process the mail daily, going through everything and acting on, filing, or tossing each item.
- Always tackle the most important task first.

- When your day is careening out of control, ask: What is the most important thing for me to do now? By assessing what needs to get done and what can wait, you can automatically prioritize.
- Important project due, and you've had it with distractions? Remove yourself. Find a quiet room and close the door.
- Can't get started? Break the project down into small steps that can be accomplished in short periods of time.
- File regularly.
- Schedule a session every six months (put it on your calendar) to weed out files (both paper and computer) and to reduce the amount of "stuff" around the office.
- Whether your telephone directory is paper or electronic, make certain you get phone numbers entered regularly so that the ones you need will always be at your fingertips.
- Keep office clutter to a minimum. Try to keep up with it nightly.

KEEP ONE EYE ON THE BIG PICTURE

One of the most difficult aspects of running your own business is that you can get lost in inconsequential details that can consume all of your time. The shop owner who refuses to leave the front of the store to step into the office to take care of business matters, the restaurant owner who keeps busy in the kitchen, or the consultant who continues to accept lower-paying clients just to keep working all mean well, but they are not taking steps that will help their businesses grow.

While part of starting your own business means that many of the details will have to be taken care of by you, it's important to plan out each day so that you keep your ultimate goal in mind and can perform the most important tasks:

- As described in the previous chapter, use a spiral or steno notebook to keep an ongoing Master List of tasks that must be done. Each day note the date, and then just keep adding to the long list of things you have to do. Each night use your Master List to plan out the following day.

- Don't schedule more than about 75 percent of your day. Running your own business guarantees that you must be prepared to interrupt your day to handle whatever crises come up.

- Choose a priority item or two to complete each day that accomplishes a broader goal for the business. Make time to put in a sales call to that big client you'd like to land; draft out a letter to the company whom you would like to have grant you exclusivity on a particular item; send out a certain number of press releases each week. These are the types of tasks that can be put off because they aren't urgent, but they are precisely the tasks that will help your business grow.

- Try to tackle your priority tasks early in the day. When interruptions occur, and they will, your schedule for the rest of the day will take a beating.

- Delegate. If you've got an assistant, use the extra help well. (Refer to Chapter 13 for information about effective delegating.) If you don't have staff, use outsiders where you can. Your accountant can handle some of your tax work that would take you hours to do; the local copy shop would be happy to photocopy and collate your presentation materials; a temp can be hired for helping out during a sale; your teenager could be put to good use helping with packing and mailing products. Don't aspire to do everything yourself!

- What's the best use of your lunchtime? Business owners often keep their noses to the grindstone, assuming that digging out from all the paperwork is the best use of their time. But what about networking with colleagues who may refer business to you, or how about entertaining a potential client? Businesses are built on relationships, and while you probably won't want to be out of the office five days per week, make certain that you're out meeting people at least twice a week. As for the occasional afternoon off to play golf with a client? Why not? The golf green is where executives from many major corporations conduct some of their business. Why not you, too?

- Keep a copy of your Business Plan handy. If you ever feel confused about the best use of your time, reread the highlights of your plan. It will remind you of what is most important in accomplishing your overall goals.

A TIME MANAGEMENT REVIEW

- Keep your office organized so that no matter what comes up, it's easy to put your hands on what you need.

- Set achievable goals to be done during your prime time.

- View projects as a series of steps rather than one big project, and write them down as such. That way you nibble away at your major goal by getting these smaller tasks taken care of.

- Give yourself deadlines for completion of your most important tasks.

- Make decisions quickly. Entrepreneurs don't have the time to revisit most issues, so do the best you can to address each thing as it comes up.

- Anticipate. Predicting what information you'll need for making a sale or thinking ahead about what to do about a potential stumbling block (a major thunderstorm may affect Sidewalk Sale Days) will help you stay on top of what is going on.

- Streamline all that you can. Establish a form e-mail or letter to be sent out to interested parties. Set up computer-generated mailing lists, order supplies in bulk through the Internet, bank electronically, and use your cell phone to return calls when you're out of the office so that they don't pile up.

- If you don't know what is happening to your time, keep a time log where you note down all that you spend time on during the day. You may learn that the phone or e-mail or other interruptions are taking up a disproportionate amount of your time, and then you can take steps to streamline or cut back.

- Learn to say "no." If you're starting your own business, you can't run the community fund-raiser this year.

- Take breaks. Stepping away from your desk/office/store for ten minutes or two hours will permit you to return feeling better prepared to tackle the project that stalled you previously.

TIME IS MONEY

You've heard this all your life, and now it definitely applies to you. It is important to make decisions that maximize your ability to build your business. This may necessitate spending money in the process:

- Hire others to do the work that is a waste of your time. Packing and shipping, photocopying, and any detail work of your business that's repetitive and time-consuming should be performed by someone else, even though you may have to hire an extra person to do it.

- Don't be penny wise and pound foolish:

— Taking clients to lunch is expensive and you can't do it all the time, but if you land a big job in the process, the money was well-spent.

— Staying over a Saturday night after a business trip saves you airfare money, but does it cost you in office productivity?

— Membership fees in professional organizations can be costly, but if it lets you do meaningful networking, it's a good investment.

— Trade publications are an additional expense, but you need to stay abreast of what is happening in your field. Borrow some issues from a colleague and evaluate which one is worth the investment.

— When considering a small job, evaluate whether or not it could lead to a bigger one. If so, it's a good investment of your time. If not, keep looking unless you're really desperate for the work.

— Keeping a low-paying client may prevent you from having the time to find a better-paying one. At some point, you'll need to cut your losses.

Managing Interruptions

Interruptions are inevitable, and many of them are necessary—the urgent call from a big client, your sales clerk who just can't handle a difficult customer, the new couch that the deliveryman has damaged—these issues will all demand your time. How can you survive despite them? The answer lies in managing the interruptions that you can so that you can cope with the ones that you can't. To begin:

- Find an interruption-free time of day to get priority work done. For most people this is early in the morning, before the store opens, or even at-home time before your kids are awake. Use your answering machine or voice mail system to cover possible phone interruptions. Once you've established a time when you're unlikely to be interrupted, be sure to use it for the important tasks. Don't fritter the time away doing small tasks that can be done later in the day.

- Interruptions are inevitable, so group the ones you know about. If office furniture is being delivered Monday afternoon, ask the air conditioning repairman to come on that day, too.

- Establish an open-door policy for staff members during a certain time of the day. If they know they can talk with you at 11 A.M., they can resist interrupting you at 10:30 A.M.

- Don't be your own worst interrupter:

- Keep your desk clear so that your eyes aren't drawn to other projects.

- When you sit down to work on something, be sure you have all that you need at your fingertips so that you needn't hop up and down for things.

- Don't take a phone call, check your e-mail, or go online when you've dedicated time to a particular project.

- Don't procrastinate. The task isn't going to go away.

MANAGING PHONE CALLS AND E-MAIL

Communicating with others is necessary and very problematic because these contacts—by phone or by e-mail—tend to interrupt other things that are going on in our lives. Here's what you need to do to manage each:

The Phone

- Use an answering machine or voice mail service so that you can control your incoming calls.

- Let staff members handle all phone calls that they can.

- Group outgoing calls. Setting aside an hour in the morning to do phoning is more efficient than making a call here and there throughout the day.

- Make notes about the issues that must be discussed. That way you won't have to call back because you forgot something.

- Write down what was discussed so that you won't forget. Client discussions should all be noted in your contact management program. Also keep a log of all telephone calls in your Master List/Office Notebook (described in the previous chapter) so if someone "forgets" details discussed, you have an accurate record of what was originally agreed to.

- When you're having difficulty reaching someone, book a telephone appointment. This saves the time wasted playing telephone tag.

- Be businesslike in your tone so that the other person will be less inclined to chat.

- Learn the art of getting off the phone:

  — "I have to leave for a meeting now, and I don't want to be late."

  — "Before we wrap up, I'd just like to make one more point . . ."

  — "We can discuss this more the next time we talk."

  — "Thank you for calling. I'll be sure to take care of it just as soon as we hang up."

E-Mail

- Check e-mail at specific times throughout the day. Don't keep hopping on and offline to check whether a new message has arrived. It fractures your time.

- Disconnect the "beep" that sounds when a new e-mail arrives. It's distracting.

- Be diligent about processing all incoming messages:

  — Delete all unwanted e-mail immediately.

  — Scan the messages and answer in order of importance.

  — Answer short messages promptly.

  — Save messages requiring research or more thought for the time of day (the beginning of the day? the end of the day?) that you set aside for processing paperwork.

  — Don't ever put into e-mail anything controversial. If a message needs some careful thought, draft the message in your regular word processing program and paste it in to an e-mail after you've had the opportunity to review it carefully.

  — Use separate Web addresses when appropriate. If you foresee receiving regular e-mail from customers, establish a separate electronic mailbox for those messages. That preserves your regular e-mail address for messages from your suppliers and other business contacts.

  — If you have a lot of customer contact via e-mail, explore the Internet services that process this exchange for you automatically.

Take Time Off

Inspiration and big ideas are a major ingredient in all businesses, and they rarely come when you're caught up in the day-to-day grind. You may not feel you have time to go to the beach on Saturday or to take a car drive to visit a friend, but these quiet times are incubators for your best ideas. Always carry a digital recorder or a pen and paper with you so that you can write down those ideas that initially you think you'll "never forget."

Keep It Simple

1. Keep yourself organized. It's the only way to run a business. You'll waste time and lose business if you can't stay on top of the details and keep focused on your priorities.

2. Don't fall prey to needless interruptions. Choose a time of the day when you can work uninterrupted and then make yourself available for the other items that need to be done.

3. Delegate when you can. As a small business owner with many responsibilities, you have to find ways to use other people to get some of the work done.

13

HIRING STAFF

AND HELPING THEM HELP YOU

WHAT'S AHEAD

Identify What You Need
Hiring Staff Members
Conducting Interviews
Look for Other Types of Help
Train Carefully
Delegate
Employee Issues
Keep Your Staff Happy

For most entrepreneurs, one of the most difficult aspects of running a business is learning to rely on staff members. Whether you've been running your business on your own for a time and are accustomed to doing everything yourself or whether you are just more comfortable when you're in total control, you share these feelings with many other people who are self-employed. It's difficult to learn to rely on others, but if you want your business to grow then you're going to need to find good employees and learn to trust them.

Maggie, a friend of mine, runs a party consulting business and her client list was growing by leaps and bounds. "Hire help," I told her, but she resisted. Then I thought of the perfect person to balance Maggie's creative side. I knew a woman with a business/accounting background who wanted to work part-time. I introduced them, Maggie hired her, and they've been working together for quite some time now. "How can I ever thank you?" says Maggie almost every time I see her.

If your business has grown and you need the help, take the plunge. You'll be glad you did.

IDENTIFY WHAT YOU NEED

"I need some help here" is not going to provide you with the help you want. Before you even consider enlarging your staff, spend a week or two writing down what types of tasks you would like someone else to do, when you would like that person available to you, and what qualities you want the person to have. By being very specific about what you're looking for, you'll be better prepared to select and hire the right person.

HIRING STAFF MEMBERS

Finding good job applicants is the first step in the hiring process. Let as many people as possible—relatives, staff members, friends, neighboring businesses—know that you want to hire someone. Often the best candidates are found through word of mouth.

Whether you post a "help wanted" ad in your shop's front window, run an ad in a local or trade newspaper, or post the job listing on the Internet, the first phase of the process is sorting through the resumés.

- The initial responses you receive to your job posting will be from the most eager candidates, but stockpile the resumés for a few days before sorting them. That way you can compare skills and select the best of the bunch.

- For entry-level jobs, weed out any people who aren't in your geographic area. With a job like flipping burgers or parking cars, the potential employee needs to be reasonably nearby, increasing the likelihood that he or she will come to work regularly. If you have a high-level managerial job for which you're interviewing, a candidate may be willing to relocate. That should be an early interview question—perhaps asked by phone before both of you waste any time pursuing the issue further.

- Be selective about the candidates you choose to interview. Then do a screening interview by phone. The person who doesn't come across well in a conversation isn't worth seeing in person.

CONDUCTING INTERVIEWS

In the 20 to 60 minutes you may spend with an applicant, you need to assess whether this person will be a help or a hindrance to you in running your business.

- Those you interview in person should have the job and the salary level redescribed to them. If they've been sending out resumés regularly, they may not recall how you originally described the job, and you don't want them talking to you under false assumptions.

- Have some sympathy for the candidate, and don't start the interview with an open-ended question like, "Tell me about yourself." How can anyone sum up what they think will get them the job in a few sentences? Instead, welcome them, and then work from the resumé and ask a question or two about some aspect of their background that interests you. This will permit the candidate to begin to feel more comfortable with you. (Imagine how nervous the person must be! Their fate is in your hands for the time being.)

- It's also a good idea to talk a bit about your ideas and goals for the company. It lets you set a tone for the interview, and having a job "discussion" is almost always more helpful to both sides than a job "grilling."

- A few standard interview questions you may want to ask include:

  — What are your strengths? (The question about "weaknesses" is often asked, but it puts the applicant in a position of trying to disguise the truth, so why ask?)

  — Tell me about a job-related accomplishment (or college-related accomplishment, if you're interviewing new graduates) about which you're very proud.

  — Is there a job-related skill you'd like to learn to do (or to do better)? If the person is applying to be your bookkeeper and expresses a desire to learn more about graphic design, you know this interview is a big mistake.

— Where do you see yourself in five years?

— Why are you interested in leaving your current job?

— From what you know of my company, what seems appealing to you about working here? If you've spent 20 minutes or more with the person and he has yet to ask any questions of you or in any other way shows a lack of ability to take interest in your company, this is a candidate who can be shown the door. The type of people who will be helpful to entrepreneurs are those with some initiative and who express an interest in helping the company run better.

- Don't ask illegal questions. Avoid age-related questions, marital status, questions concerning care of children, weight issues, or any sort of question that could be considered discriminatory. If you would like an applicant to have a certain level of education, put that in the job description so that it's written in as a requirement (and it must be a reasonable requirement; requesting that a handyperson have a college education could get you into trouble because it isn't really necessary).

- Interview candidates in whom you're interested at least twice, and if you have other staff members let one of them sit in on one of the interviews. A return visit is likely to make the person relax a bit, and his/her remarks should be increasingly enthusiastic about the position.

- The more relaxed the applicant the better the opportunity you'll have to judge whether or not the person is a "fit" for your company. Do you feel comfortable with this person? Will other staff members like this candidate? (In a small company, harmony is an important issue.)

- Ask for references and *check them.* To get the most out of a call to a reference, describe the work the person will be doing and ask about any specific concerns you have about his ability to do the job. You may be surprised at what you learn.

- Tempted as you may be to hire the slick job seeker with the terrific resumé, remain focused on the job for which you're hiring, and try to select the best person for that job. The "been there, done that" candidate may have a great background, but is that going to be the person who can be trained to be your assistant and back you up?

- If you have solicited applications via advertising, you are required to keep those applications on file for a year. In the file of applications, make notes regarding the criteria used in selecting the final candidate.

LOOK FOR OTHER TYPES OF HELP

While most businesses eventually need to put people on staff, there are also other ways to get the help you need. The fewer people you have on payroll (or the longer you wait before you have to add staff), the fewer your accounting responsibilities and tax obligations.

What businesses in your town already exist that could help you out?

- Temporary employment agencies now place a full range of employees, from lawyers and accountants right through to the traditional secretaries and assistants. Call one in your area and discuss your needs. For the fee paid, they handle all the paperwork and tax headaches, and you have no long-term commitment to the person. When the job is done, the employee simply returns to the temp agency roster.

- Advertising agencies will manage your advertising for a fee, and a freelance publicist will handle publicity for you.

- Copy shops not only copy but can put together presentation materials; the independent mail business can handle packing and shipping of moderate amounts of merchandise; there are full-scale fulfillment houses that will store and ship major amounts of merchandise.

- If your business requires a "real" person to cover your phone, consider using an answering service—even in this day of voice mail these services still exist.
- Cleaning services work as independent contractors, so don't even think of pushing a broom yourself if you feel the upkeep of your space has gotten ahead of you.

TRAIN CAREFULLY

- For at least the first week, be certain that you or a staff member are in close touch with your new employee. The "sink or swim" method of employee management will spell an unpleasant ending for the relationship. The best workers are those who understand exactly how you want business conducted.

- Spell out your expectations and outline what will make an employee eligible for raises and bonuses. The person who understands how you evaluate performance is more likely to live up to your expectations.

DELEGATE

"It will take less time if I just do it myself" is one main reason people give me when I suggest they should delegate more to their staff or outsiders. While the ideal helper is one who arrives knowing exactly how to do the tasks you need done, this isn't very likely to happen. For that reason, it's important that you consider training very much a part of delegating:

- Teach the job at a time when you're less likely to be interrupted—otherwise the training session will seem to go on for hours.

- Explain the job and show exactly how you want it done.

- Note down the steps of the job so there are set guidelines to follow. This will make it easier to teach it to someone else.

- Perform the job together (opening and processing the mail?) the first time or two. Then let the person do it on his or her own with you doing a final check.

- Follow up. Note dates on both your calendars when the two of you should meet. If you've delegated tasks that need to be completed for a presentation you're giving, you don't want to find out too late that the staff person hasn't kept up with the pace.

- Over time, you should be able to delegate and give the person only a "due date." Note that date in your calendar so that tasks aren't forgotten.

- Compliment the worker on a job well done, and be sure to show appreciation if the efforts of the staff member made you look particularly good when giving a speech or a presentation.

EMPLOYEE ISSUES

- Investigate employee benefits such as health insurance and retirement programs. If you expect to grow—and expect to be around for a long time—then you'll attract better employees if you can offer these types of benefits. Health care has become so expensive that some job seekers pay more attention to the benefits package offered than they do to the salary. Finding affordable plans isn't easy but they are out there, and you will benefit as well if you can link up with a program now and get coverage for yourself and your staff.

- Compensation for your staff should be close to or above the going rate for the type of work they are doing. Don't be cheap about increases. Particularly in the current employment market, if you don't reward an employee and keep him at a competitive salary level, you'll soon find that the time you've spent training your staff member will benefit someone else who is willing to pay him more.

- Be clear about employee policies. Decide on issues such as holidays, time off, overtime, sick days, and other benefits. Check with entrepreneurs running similar businesses, the SBA, or other resources listed in Chapter 4.

- Establish a schedule for employee performance reviews. By giving a person feedback on their work, you'll establish a way to reinforce the positive and smooth out some of the negative traits of an employee.

- Establish and enforce clear policies on employee theft and substance abuse. According to the U.S. Chamber of Commerce, one out of three business failures can be attributed to employee theft. No employee should have sole responsibility for approving expenses, cutting checks, and keeping books. These jobs should be divided so that you have a check-and-balance system.

- As mentioned in Chapter 10, talk to your accountant about a new staff member, and let your accountant or an outside service manage the payroll and the withholding and payment of appropriate taxes.

KEEP YOUR STAFF HAPPY

- Treat your staff like people you care about. This seems obvious, but sometimes entrepreneurs are so caught up with growing their businesses that they neglect to give a kind word to the people who are helping the business grow. By showing some personal interest and concern in each person, you'll begin to build loyalty.

- Praise jobs well done.

- Offer an opportunity for feedback. Your staff member may have created a more efficient way for processing something. Be the type of boss with whom she or he can share this new idea.

- When you can, be flexible about personal time off or unusual work hours. Employers who can permit staff members to take care of personal needs are almost always rewarded by loyalty and devotion from the employee.

 KEEP IT SIMPLE

1. Try to use independent contractors and outside services for as long as you can. The longer you can hold off on adding staff, the less time you will have to spend on employee-related issues.

2. Once you decide it's time to hire someone, think through the job carefully. Spread the word that you're looking so that you'll have a healthy number of candidates from which to choose.

3. Once you hire an employee, invest quality time in training the person. Give positive feedback and retrain when something isn't being done properly. If you've selected a good person, he or she is worth the effort.

PART FIVE

BUILDING YOUR BUSINESS

14

MARKETING AND SALES

WHAT'S AHEAD

Creating a Marketing Plan
How Can You Reach Customers and Potential Customers?
The Importance of Targeting Your Market
Budgeting for Expanding Your Market
Cost per Customer
Bringing in Customers
Selling Yourself and Your Business

've had the opportunity to know some businesswomen who were absolutely first-rate at promoting their businesses:

- Melanie had created a line of makeup products, and she felt that publicity and a high profile was the way to the top of her field. Every time I talked to her, she had a new reason to contact beauty editors, and she just didn't stop. Today her line is internationally known.

- Francis wanted to sell her services to public relations people, so she didn't bother with the press. She went directly to the people who could hire her. She created specialty postcards, and made it a priority to stay in touch with a targeted group of PR professionals whom she felt would hire her. Today she runs a successful business and has more clients than she needs.

- Personal visibility at local society events and a major commitment to networking were Jane's methods for drumming up clients for her new interior design business. As a woman with a great sense of personal style, Jane was soon being photographed everywhere. As she became well known, she began to be hired by clients who in turn have spread the word about her design services.

- As a meetings and events planner, Carol found that donating her services at the right times and for the right organizations has been key to finding paying clients. By organizing charitable events once or twice per year that are attended by company executives and nonprofit leaders, she's been able to build her business in just the way she'd always wanted.

Once you go into business for yourself, your single most important task is selling your product and services. The forerunner to successful sales is a strong marketing program, and taking the time to plan out your avenues of approach will save you both time and money.

The decisions and planning you read about in this chapter will help you focus on all types of selling—from in-person meetings to using e-mail to finding future customers through advertising and publicity, which are discussed here and in Chapter 15.

CREATING A MARKETING PLAN

One of the benefits of having prepared a business plan is that some of the work of your marketing plan has already been done. To prepare your marketing plan, refer back to the work you did in Chapter 2 in preparing your business plan:

Define Your Business
- What is your product or service?
- What makes it unique?

- What is your competition?

- Identify your niche of the market. (You may be selling high-end ski wear; your market is the person who may care more about looking good *by* the slopes, not necessarily on them. Selling to the fashionable customer is very different from marketing to the rugged outdoorsperson.)

Define Your Customers

(If you're just starting out, then these answers may need to be speculative, or you may have some early experience on which to base your answers.)

- Who is your current customer?

- How do they learn of your product or service?

- What do they value most about it?

- What group would you like to target next as potential customers?

HOW CAN YOU REACH CUSTOMERS AND POTENTIAL CUSTOMERS?

- Can current customers be used to sell to new customers? (Is there a way to encourage word of mouth?)

- Will your current method of reaching customers also work to reach new people?

- Prioritize the following list of ways to communicate with customers. Think about how they can be most useful to you:

  _____ Yellow Page ads and listings

  _____ Publicity

  _____ Internet Web site and Web links from other sites

  _____ Display advertising

  Specify where _____

  _____ Co-op advertising (with a supplier)

  _____ Point-of-sale selling

  _____ Direct marketing

  Specify telephone, mail, e-mail, other _____

  _____ Special promotions (contests, seminars, special events)

- Brainstorm with staff or friends for new ways to market your business.

THE IMPORTANCE OF TARGETING YOUR MARKET

Inevitably I'll meet someone who will share with me how their product is just the thing for everyone. "Anybody could wear the rain slickers I'm making . . ." Well, that may be true, but a sure way to fail in business is to decide that your market is the "entire world."

Though one day you may run a company big enough to sell to almost anyone almost anywhere, the smart entrepreneur captures his market segment by segment. Why? Because by narrowing your target you increase the likelihood of getting your message across.

To return to the example of the rain slicker, why not aim at getting it on the backs of as many college students as you can? And if you still are limited by distribution (currently you are only distributing in the Southeast), then be even more specific: College students in the South Atlantic states. But let's not waste time at the tiny schools, start by aiming for the students in the larger university towns.

By making these decisions, you can easily answer the following questions:

— Where should you place ads?

University newspapers in the South Atlantic states, or on radio stations that reach those markets.

— Where would you run promotions?

On larger campuses in that geographic region.

— If you were to try to publicize your slickers, what newspapers and magazines would you approach?

Those read by the students in the stated area.

— If you wanted to target e-mail messages, what type of list would you be looking for?

College students in the above region.

As you can see, narrowing your focus makes it possible to do a better job of reaching a specific group. Once you feel you've saturated that market, you can try to broaden your outreach, at which point you can make a new series of decisions based on your experience:

— Do you want to continue to reach college students only? If so, you can work on increasing your distribution and start marketing to a broader geographic market.

— Or do you want to start appealing to high school students (and younger) in the geographic area you've identified?

A good marketing program is a lot like getting organized—the more you break things down into manageable parts, the easier it is to handle.

BUDGETING FOR EXPANDING YOUR MARKET

According to the SBA, the two main reasons small businesses fail is because they underestimate the amount of capital required, and they don't consider how they will actually market their product or services. Therefore, it is *vital* to the future of your business that you earmark some money for marketing your product or services. Later on, your marketing funds will be a percentage of sales.

When setting your budget, consider:

— What is the size of your market and where are these people located?

If you need a national market it will be far more expensive to reach them than if you're targeting a local market or a specific industry.

— What kind of marketing is involved?

Even if you're aiming at a local market, it's more expensive to create a television commercial than it is to have a print ad designed.

— What kind of sales tools will be effective?

Will a simple brochure and a Web site be enough to sell your services? Some businesses will need to invest in four-color presentation folders with full-color photographs; a business consultant may need to prepare a Power Point presentation to be shown to prospects.

- What marketing methods are within your current budget?

- How will you test and measure results?

COST PER CUSTOMER

Over time you will want to develop ways to measure the effectiveness of your marketing. How many customers did an ad bring in? How many people visit your Web site? Did a large number of people hear you interviewed on a radio program? (The news coverage is free, but your publicity program does cost time and money.)

If a $500 ad brought in five customers who each spent $50, it cost you $100 per customer to sell $50 worth of merchandise. The wise businessperson is probably contemplating pulling that ad quickly before more money is lost, but don't be too hasty. First of all, an ad needs to run several times before you can measure its effectiveness. (See Chapter 15 for more information about advertising.) What's more, if you run a day spa and those five customers came in for a facial one month, and a facial and manicure the next month, and a massage the following month, then that $500 was well spent. You have to consider the nature of your business. Some businesses, like a store that specializes in vacuum cleaners, have to keep looking for more and more customers because repeat customers don't need to come back very often. Observe your overall sales pattern before making firm decisions on how well you're doing spending your marketing money.

BRINGING IN CUSTOMERS

Sometimes business owners get started with a good idea, make some initial sales, and then find that no one comes into the store (or calls the consultant) again. Part of your job in bringing in customers involves marketing, but part of it is running a top-flight business. There are four basic elements that can make a difference in whether or not your business is valued by past and future customers:

1. **Inventory (or for a consultant, advice).** Consistency is very important in running a business. Can you remain fully stocked with a good quality of whatever it is the preteen set, for example, keeps coming into your store to buy? If you run out, your customers lose their reasons for coming in. Or if a parent takes your recommendation and buys a computer game that his child loves, he'll come back to you for another product and another idea. Consultants have to remain tuned in and in top form for offering smart advice. You're only as good as your last idea.

2. **Price.** Whether you're selling your services as a consultant or running a flower store where you must price all of your flowers, you need to establish a strategy for pricing—and surprisingly, you don't always have to offer the lowest price in order to bring in business. First, you need to know how your competition charges. If someone in the market is already offering "rock bottom" prices, and they really are rock bottom, then you can't start a business and charge less. Based on this information, the flower store might actually decide to position itself as the "upscale" flower store, and if this positioning is done successfully, then the store can afford to charge more for what will probably be more exotic cuts of flowers and very artistic arrangements. Customers won't mind paying higher prices because they'll feel the flowers are worth it.

3. **Service.** As a consultant, you may offer "hand-holding" service where you really are available to a client almost 'round the clock, or a store may offer services such as calling certain customers as soon as special products arrive. Level of service expected by the customer is determined by product positioning. The lower your price, the less value a customer places on service, understanding that to save money she may need to pick it up or assemble it herself.

4. **Delivery.** Does the customer receive the product in the fashion and at the price he expects, depending on how you've positioned your business? The pricey gourmet grocery in Manhattan may offer "within-the-hour" free delivery for phone orders, and their delivery people may be dressed in uniform. The knock-down furniture store with extraordinarily low prices may expect customers to pull around to the back of the store to pick up merchandise. Or the auto parts company that can guarantee overnight delivery to the companies serviced may beat out competition from the businesses where delivery takes 48 hours. Delivery can be a competitive advantage, and at the very least, your method of delivery needs to be consistent with customer expectations.

Features such as fair pricing (according to your positioning in the marketplace), top-quality service, speedy delivery, and complete inventory are the types of business elements that will keep customers coming back again and again.

SELLING YOURSELF AND YOUR SBUSINESS

Some entrepreneurs are really good at what they do, but they dislike the "selling" aspect of running a business, or they dislike being thought of as a "salesperson." Yet there are a couple of things to keep in mind when it comes to putting your best "sales" foot forward:

- The qualities of truly good salespeople are actually wonderful human qualities. While the superslick sales type may make some big sales, those who really excel at it are smart and caring people:

  — They are great listeners—*important in determining exactly what a customer needs.*

  — They genuinely care about their products—*just as you do, or you wouldn't have started a business.*

  — They care about their customers, and their prime focus is on being of service, not totally on making the sale—*a personality who wants to please others has the best chance of doing so, and making the sale.*

  — They don't personalize rejection—*it takes a lot of effort to get a business up and running, and you'll find you'll have more energy for pressing forward if you don't let business missteps get you down.*

In addition, here's some advice:

- Work in the arena in which you are most comfortable. One financial consultant hated making cold calls, disliking the one-on-one opportunity for someone to turn him down, but he was a dynamic speaker. He found that by investing time in speaking to community organizations and businesses—and providing his audience with real value—he began to find new clients. Eventually word of mouth about his services began to spread, and he had to begin cutting down on speaking engagements in order to have time to service all his clients.

- Remember that no one makes 100 percent of the sales he or she wants to. Go into each situation assuming that you will learn something from the experience. You may get feedback about your service or product, or learn information about the potential client that may not be useful immediately, but can serve as a reason to call the client back in a few months.

- Be persistent, in a pleasant way. People like to do business with people they know. If you get a lead on a client you'd like, keep finding ways to stay in touch and build familiarity.

- Knowledge, practice, and a confident attitude are keys to making a positive impression. If things aren't going well, revisit your product (or service) and rethink the customer benefits, practice with friends and relatives, and remain confident. Countless entrepreneurs can tell long tales of rejection after rejection (after long nights creating new product or assembling more sales literature—no one said this would be easy), but they just kept selling, and eventually their business became an "overnight success."

- Take time to understand a customer's needs and show how your product or service satisfies them. *Selling* your product is not the point; *showing how your product satisfies the customer's needs is what will get you a sale.*

- Position yourself as a "problem solver." Whether you're selling a product or providing a service, make certain that your product minimizes hassles in a customer's life rather than creates them. The product that is difficult to assemble; the lamp that requires imported lightbulbs; the mailing service that packs some of the direct mail improperly—all these *create* problems for the customer. You will sell again and again if you stay on top of the process so that the customer's life is better for having done business with you.

- Appeal to their emotions. While you start the sales process with logic, the ultimate decision is made emotionally, so discuss with the person the end benefits of having made the contemplated purchase.

- Offer a "wow!" If a customer is skeptical, show how much you believe in your product: "If this sound system isn't everything you'd hoped for, I will send someone out to pick it up and give you a refund check."

- Stop talking so you can listen carefully. In the process you may learn enough to clinch the sale, or you may receive feedback that permits you to change your tactics for the next time.

- Give people more than their money's worth. One well-known knife company always has special items that their salesperson can add in for "free," depending on the size of the sale. This builds goodwill and customers will feel they have gotten a particularly good deal.

- Think of interesting ways to draw attention to your store or your product and generate media attention. For example, a storybook character could visit a children's book or clothing shop (you rent a costume and one of your clerks wears it), which could be a good customer draw. (See the next chapter for more on this idea.)

- Be creative with your products. If you sell baby products and the gorilla at the zoo has just given birth to twins, are there items you could donate (in pairs, of course) that could be used in the gorilla nursery?

- Be creative in your selling. If someone's grandson "just loved" the books you recommended for his last birthday, then take time to think of new books for your customer to send to him this year.

- A turndown isn't a permanent "no." It's an opportunity to try to learn more about your customer and how to better solve his problems.

- Keep your promises. Whatever you've said you'll do in the process of making the sale is exactly what you must deliver.

- Keep up to date on sales materials and techniques. Consider asking a friend to critique your presentation, and visit these sites for additional information on sales materials and face-to-face selling: *www.salesdoctors.com*, *www.sales.com*, and *www.footinthedoor.com*.

KEEP IT SIMPLE

1. Creating a thoughtful marketing plan is very important to building your business. Take the time to do the necessary research and planning so that you know where you're going with your business.

2. Most effective marketing programs target only a segment of a market. It's more affordable and effective to aim for each group one at a time. Eventually you can market to an increasingly larger audience.

3. The people who are best at selling their product, their services, or their business to others are those who genuinely believe in what they have to say and take the time to listen to the customer. By combining those two factors, a good salesperson will be able to show a potential customer how the product or service will solve his or her problems.

15

ADVERTISING AND PUBLICITY

WHAT'S AHEAD

Your Advertising Program
Creating an Ad
Radio and TV Advertising
Advertising on the Web
Tracking Your Ad Results
Easy Access Keeps Sales Strong
How to Build Business Through Free Publicity
What Is Publicity?
Identifying Your News Value
The Press Release

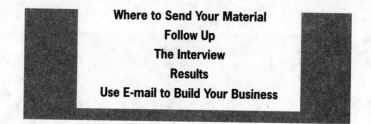

As you've learned in the previous chapter, you can't build a business by sitting in your chair waiting for customers to come to you. Whether you're selling computer systems, hair ornaments, or real estate, or trying to bring customers to your dance studio, your antique store, or your Internet site, advertising and publicity are two valuable methods for locating new customers and reminding previous customers to come back to you.

YOUR ADVERTISING PROGRAM

Much of the information you're going to need to establish an advertising program is information you've already considered when preparing your marketing plan (as in Chapter 14). To run an effective ad campaign, you need to:

— Have a strong concept of what is unique about your product or business.

- Know the demographics of your customers (age, gender, geographic area).

- Have general ideas of where you can reach them (newspapers, in-flight magazines, fliers distributed at the local gym club in town, radio advertising, the Internet, or the Yellow Pages).

- Once you have this information, you are ready to plan your advertising program. The first step is deciding on the best method for reaching your customers and potential customers (you won't be able to afford all the publications they read or radio or TV stations they follow).

- Demographics provide the information you need when making that decision. Here's how to learn about the demographics of the various publications and programs you're considering:

  - Each medium you're considering (newspaper, magazine, radio, TV, the Internet) will have ad representatives who can discuss the demographics of your audience with you. Call publications or programs that interest you and ask for their media kit. It will provide you with some sample copies of a print publication as well as a lot of information about the audience they reach.

  - Visit the library and look at the *Standard Rate and Data Service* directories, also available online at *http://srds.com*. The directories list publications by type as well as the audiences they reach, and if you're considering any type of national advertising, these are good reference tools.

- Sometimes you'll find specialty publications or sections of a newspaper that consumers regularly check if they are interested in a specific product. If you run a carpet store, then the "home" section of your newspaper may be the place where "everyone" in the business advertises; if you sell electronics, there may be a special section of the Sunday paper where your ad needs to be. If people wait to read certain ad sections before buying a particular category of product, then you definitely want to have your ad in with the competition. (Publications that are followed for particular information are called "search corridors.")

- If you're still unsure where to advertise, talk to your customers. If you sell business to business, a customer may remind you of a trade magazine you hadn't thought of. If you sell to a local area, you may learn about a "pennysaver" publication that people actually follow for certain information.

- Don't let an ad rep talk you into spending money speculatively. Be certain the demographics they describe match up with your customers. Advertising is expensive, and you need to spend your money where it will count.

CREATING AN AD

- Decide what message you want to convey. Do you want to advertise a special sale? A special product? Create a special image through the ads that you run?

- Ad reps at local publications may offer to help you create an ad—it's in their best interests to do so. Their help may consist of your working with someone on their staff, or it may involve being referred to an outside agency, but in any case, they are unlikely to turn you down if you need help creating an ad.

- Decide exactly what the particular ad under discussion is going to say. Ads must be succinct and to the point.

  — Your ad should attract attention. Whether it's an attention-grabbing headline or a unique graphic design, create an ad that people will notice.

  — The ad should appeal to the reader and offer benefits. "Save money," "enhance your lifestyle," "have more free time," "the vacation of a lifetime" are all promising benefits. Another tactic is to present news: "bold new way to take care of fleas and ticks," "timesaving method for cleaning your home," "revolutionary way to ease back pain . . ."

  — The ad should answer, "Why should the consumer buy the product from me?" In a small ad this is difficult to do, but "convenient" or "low-priced" or "open 24 hours" are all short, descriptive phrases that answer the question and may encourage customers to come to you.

— Motivate readers, listeners, or viewers: Are you offering something free to the first one hundred customers? Is your store having a half-off sale for a limited time? You've got to give them a reason to make you a priority.

• Once you have your ad, be prepared to run it several times. The ad rep is going to tell you that you're going to have to buy several ads before you know if the ad itself is any good. Unfortunately for your pocketbook, he's right. Readers, listeners, and viewers are drawn in over time—they need to become familiar with your message before they are likely to respond to it. For that reason, your ad dollars are better spent advertising in one or two mediums rather than using a scattershot method and buying a little advertising everywhere.

RADIO AND TV ADVERTISING

Small businesses are often nervous about getting involved with radio and TV because they fear it will be too costly. However, you may find that the effectiveness of radio or TV for your business makes this form of media important to explore.

- Both radio and TV personnel will be helpful in assisting you with the creation of an ad. Radio stations will often assemble a commercial for free, while TV stations usually charge for production time (prices range from $300 to $2,000). Call the stations that seem logical for reaching your target market and see what they can offer.

- Talk to the sales manager about demographics and what time of day you would like to advertise. Then check ads and programming during that time, and see what types of ads are running then. Do they appeal to the market you're trying to reach?

- Ask the sales personnel to show you information from rating services like Arbitron or Nielsen so that you can calculate how much it will cost you to reach your target audience.

- Even with a tight budget, it is possible to create a "quality" commercial for radio or television. If either of these mediums offer the best way to reach your target market, get the help you need in doing so.

ADVERTISING ON THE WEB

Even if you have a product that is perfect for Web surfers, hold off for a time on paying for ads on the Internet. Click-through (response) rates on banner ads is currently a dismal .5 percent, meaning that there is still a lot to be learned about placing ads on the Internet.

A good Web site and any publicity you can get on Internet information sites are your best paths for attracting the attention of the Web crowd.

TRACKING YOUR AD RESULTS

When you start a business you can't afford to waste money, so it's important to know when you're spending your money wisely and when it's going down the drain. To track your ad results, try the following:

- Feature a specific product in only one of your ads. Then if you notice an increase in sales of that product, you'll know your ad is working.

- Place an identifying mark on ads in different publications. Then offer customers a discount for bringing in the ad. You'll instantly know which ad is bringing results.

- Keep in mind that consumers need to become familiar with your ad (often they need to see it as many as nine times) before responding to it. After the ad has been running for a time, see how your sales results are.

- Stop running a long-running ad and see if there is a difference in your business.

- When customers call or come in, ask how they heard about you. You may get some surprising answers—like one customer who responded to an ad from two years ago!

- As you gather information about the effectiveness of your ads, consider how much it costs to capture each customer from that ad. (Refer to Chapter 14.)

- Pay attention to the effectiveness of your advertising so that you can be certain your ad dollars are well spent.

EASY ACCESS KEEPS SALES STRONG

Have you ever responded to an ad as a customer only to find that the phone number was constantly busy, or when you stopped by the store for their special offer on grass seed they were sold out? What are these business owners thinking? Once you make an offer via an ad or publicity, you have to expect—and prepare for—a response. Whether it's having enough phone lines (or carefully managing the ones you have by calling people back if there's a frantic rush), or making certain you have enough stock, be sure you live up to your advertised (or publicized) promises.

HOW TO BUILD BUSINESS THROUGH FREE PUBLICITY

Publicity is one of the most valuable tools a business owner has for building interest in his or her company, and those of you who have had experience with this type of exposure surely know its value. Some businesses have been launched on publicity alone; others see direct sales results from a mention in the newspaper; and still others talk about the heightened visibility press coverage gives them.

Publicity has been vital to my consulting business through the years. People would much prefer to hire a consultant they've read about instead of a consultant whose ad they've seen. My series of books on organizing have also been sold primarily through publicity. I jump at every opportunity I have to talk about any aspect of time management or organization, and it certainly sells books.

WHAT IS PUBLICITY?

Publicity is free media exposure. It may take the form of a story on the television news, a radio interview, or an article in a newspaper or magazine. You provide the media with information about your business or service, and they decide how best to use the material within their program or publication.

Though some business owners find they can rely totally on publicity in promoting their businesses, most find that publicity acts as a perfect complement to other forms of marketing. If potential customers read an article about your business, they start watching for your ads, pay more attention to your literature, and may soon drop in or call to try your product or service.

In addition, there are two main benefits to publicity: credibility and cost. If you gain mention on radio, TV, or in print, it is, in effect, editorial recommendation. An unbiased observer (the reporter or interviewer) is saying that you are worthy of notice. To the reader or viewer this greatly enhances your credibility.

In general, there are four basic steps for getting started (each of which will be covered in detail):

1. Identify what you want to say to the public.

2. Write it up in a simple press release—the accepted format for approaching the press.

3. Send the release to the members of the media who are likely to be interested in the information.

4. Follow up! Follow up! Follow up!!!

There's really not much more to it. The same process is simply repeated again and again in order to keep your name in the public eye.

IDENTIFYING YOUR NEWS VALUE

When you see an interview on television or read an article about a business in the newspaper, there is always something of specific interest to the public: a special event is about to take place, a unique product is now available, the business has won an award, the business owner has overcome great odds in order to succeed, or sometimes, the business owner is offering specific advice on how to do something.

In some cases, business owners "create" news by holding special events or donating goods or services to a worthy cause. A logical tie-in for pet-related businesses might be sponsoring a dog-and-owner walkathon to raise funds for a local cause. People stopping by to pick up information on the dog walkathon would build traffic and eventually lead to more business.

You may already have something specific to announce about your business: news of a trunk show being held in your store; the fact that you are now the sole distributor of a certain type of computer speaker or that you or your organization has won some type of award; or perhaps that you are relocating to expanded quarters. Here are some possible ideas for press coverage for various types of businesses:

— Advice from a business consultant on how to hire and keep good employees.

— Advice on topics ranging from rabies to fleas from a veterinarian trying to launch his business.

— Suggestions on what to look for in a quality mattress from a bedding company.

THE PRESS RELEASE

A press release is the best method of conveying your message to the media (see below for suggestions on writing it). As you prepare it, keep in mind the following questions:

1. Who are your customers (past, present, and potential)? This will help you determine to whom you should direct the information. If you want to promote new takeout dinners for working parents, then you want to "make news" in the media directed to that audience.

2. What media are these people likely to read, watch, or listen to? The names and addresses of these publications and programs become your press mailing list.

The format of a press release is designed to be easy to read and quickly assessed. Since the press release is an important part of your publicity program, it's worth devoting time to. If you're not comfortable writing it yourself, hire someone or get a friend to help you.

All press releases contain the following elements:

1. **Who to contact for more information.** The name, address, and telephone number of this person (likely you or a staff member) goes at the top of the page, along with any company logo or icon.

2. **Release date.** Most are "For Immediate Release."

3. **Headline.** This should be a factual, sometimes clever, summary of what the release is about.

4. **Body of the release.** The release is written in the "inverted pyramid" style—a term you may recall from high school English class. All vital details (who, what, when, where, why) are given in a short first paragraph, while all other details are provided in descending order of importance. A release should conclude with information about what the public should do if interested: call for more information, buy tickets at the door, etc.

Press releases should be written simply and clearly. Sentences and paragraphs should be kept short. Glowing description should be avoided.

Once written, the release should be typed (double-spaced) and if it runs more than one page (it should only be two at the most), the pages should be stapled together. And remember the point of the release: to be attractive and interesting to the editor. Be sure that the copy looks good and is easy to read. The release represents you, and it should do justice to the type of businessperson you are.

WHERE TO SEND YOUR MATERIAL

While your story might not be the type of subject covered by *Time*, there are plenty of other publications that do write about stories like yours. Believe it or not, they'll be glad to hear from you! The key is in properly identifying which publications and programs will be most receptive. Consider the following:

- Does the publication or program generally deal with stories such as the one you have in mind? (If your local paper never publicizes new products, it isn't going to start now.)

- If an article appears there, will you get new customers? In other words, are its readers or viewers potential customers? (This will help you set priorities. You might be able to get publicity in a magazine in the next county, but if their readership isn't likely to travel to your county, then start close to home first.)

- Once you've identified the publication, get the name of a specific person to whom to send your release. If your material belongs with the lifestyle section of the paper, find out the name of an editor or writer and send the material directly to that person. Phone the operator for help, or with magazines, consult the masthead. With radio and TV, you'll need the name of the producer or talent coordinator.

FOLLOW UP

Follow up with a phone call after sending the material. Don't be pushy, and don't ask for a specific commitment, but do check to see if they've received the material and whether they thought they could use it.

THE INTERVIEW

If the reporter plans to use your press release, you're all set. However, if an interview will be involved, make a few notes as to what you will say. For example, if the topic is how to plan a wedding, come up with a few specific tips and write them down. That way you will make your points clearly, and for the reporter to report accurately.

Also develop a one- or two-sentence summary of what your business is, and then make a list of several positive points about your product or service. That way you won't be caught short if the interviewer starts out by saying, "Well, tell me about your business."

RESULTS

While there are clipping services for newspapers, magazines, and even Internet stories, you'll hear about most of the publicity you receive when people call, come in, or send checks.

In the long run, you'll soon find that publicity breeds publicity. The local radio host will read the story about you in the newspaper, and out of the blue, you'll get a call from the radio station. Ultimately, you'll find that publicity is a great way to create new business.

USE E-MAIL TO BUILD YOUR BUSINESS

The Internet has solved a major problem of small businesses—that of communication and visibility. Now for the first time there is a fast and easy way to be in touch with your customers and potential customers to update them on your business.

- E-mail today is an essential way of doing business. If you need a quick response from a client or a customer, then a quick electronic message almost always nets you the information you want.

- Use e-mail for customer reminders:

  — People will appreciate hearing from you if you have an important message for them, such as a reminder that their dog is due for a rabies shot. In this case, e-mail can replace the mailed postcard, an item that is frequently lost by the postal system and often misplaced by the recipient.

— If you run a garden store, an e-mail can remind customers that it's time for spring planting and can describe the new plants you have available. Unsolicited e-mail is just as unpopular as junk mail, but many people like to be placed on mailing lists of stores they care about, so if you ask, they may actually request that they hear from you.

— Offer people a way *not* to hear from you. If your messages are viewed as time-wasters and are deleted the instant they are viewed by a recipient, then you're actually building up negative feelings in that person. Provide them with an e-mail address they can use to get off your mailing list. If they really are a hot prospect, you'll find other ways to sell to them.

• Don't send large files or attachments unless invited to do so. There's nothing more irritating than receiving an e-mail that takes a long time to open or download. This is counterproductive for your business.

• Save time by using e-mail to do business with your vendors. A quick message to a vendor is much more efficient than trying to reach him by phone.

• Use the Web for research. Anything you want to know is only a few clicks away. Be persistent.

KEEP IT SIMPLE

1. Advertising and publicity are important to any business. They can extend your outreach to new customers and remind old customers to return to you. Be sure to set aside both time and money and make promoting your business a regular part of your work day.

2. You need to place your ads carefully. Don't waste money advertising in a publication that doesn't reach your target market, even if the sales rep is a nice guy. You need to watch your marketing dollars closely and be certain they are carefully spent.

3. Publicity offers credibility that an ad never can. In running a story about you, a reporter or editor brings you to the attention of his or her readers. Publicity is an editorial endorsement and a particularly effective way of promoting your business.

CONCLUSION

GROWING BIGGER

The primary purpose of this book is to help you launch your business start-up. Before ending the book, I would like to take this opportunity to share some knowledge I've gained from working with business owners over a long period of time:

Don't grow bigger until you're forced to.

In my work I help people get organized and regain control of their lives, and I know all too well that when people become overwhelmed, it often causes them to fail. By forcing yourself to stay small (don't rent the space next door to expand your retail store just because it's available; don't add a full-time employee because you "need some extra help"; don't take on a new line of products just because it's offered to you), you can increase your opportunity to be profitable. Larger space, more employees, and a more extensive product line all cost more money, so you have to increase business just to cover the bottom line.

When it is time to grow bigger—and with luck, there *will be* that time—plan your expansion just as carefully as you did your start-up. Go back through the book and rethink the chapters, keeping in mind the new potential offered by your new size. Map out exactly how you will conduct business once you are larger.

If you have created a successful start-up and plan your expansion carefully, your newly expanded business can be just as profitable as your start-up because you did it carefully and built your business the right way.

ABOUT THE AUTHORS

RONNI EISENBERG, author of *Organize Yourself!*, has given a multitude of workshops, lectures, and demonstrations across the country on how to get organized. She lives and works in Westport, Connecticut, with her husband and three children.

KATE KELLY, who co-authors Ronni's books, is a professional writer who owns and operates her own publishing business. She lives in Westchester County, New York, with her husband and three children.